The Cold Blue Sky

The Cold Blue Sky

A B-17 Gunner in World War Two

Jack Novey

Edited and with an Introduction by Fryar Calhoun

Howell Press

Printed in the United States of America

Howell Press
1147 River Road, Suite 2
Charlottesville, Virginia 22901

Library of Congress Cataloging in Publication Data

Novey, Jack.
    The cold blue sky: a B-17 gunner in World War Two / Jack
Novey ; edited and with an introduction by Fryar Calhoun.
    p. cm.
    Includes index.
    ISBN: 1-57427-066-4
    LCCN: 96-080035

    1. Novey, Jack. 2. United States. Army Air Forces—Biogra-
phy. 3. World War, 1939-1945—Aerial operations, American.
4. World War, 1939-1945—Personal narratives, American.
I. Title.

D790.N68 1997   940.54'4973
                                   QBI96-2571

Frontispiece: Dawn finds B-17s of the 96th Bomb
Group over the North Sea on the way to Germany.
(96th Bomb Group Museum/Geoff Ward)

*This book is dedicated with love to my wife Daniella
and with respect and honor to the memory of my comrades in arms
of the Eighth Air Force and the 96th Bomb Group
who gave their lives in the war*

Foreword

When World War Two ended, I felt incredibly lucky to have survived. I closed the door on the past and rarely thought or talked about the war for thirty years and more. Then a chance occurrence, related in the last chapter of this book, brought my war memories flooding back. I began to seek out my old comrades in arms and to attend Eighth Air Force reunions.

I began to feel a strange compulsion to tell my story, and finally I sat down and wrote it. True, World War Two was a long time ago, and the United States has fought two long wars and one short one since then. But even if my story is just a footnote in history, I felt duty bound to relate it, if for no other audience than my children and perhaps their children.

The bomber and fighter pilots have told their stories. The aces and the colonels, the generals and the war historians—all of them have told their versions of the air war over Europe. I hope you will indulge me as I tell you my own war story. Like most of the guys in the bomber crews, I was an enlisted man—a sergeant and gunner. Unlike most of them, I somehow survived a full tour of combat duty, twenty-five missions.

Most autobiographies signify the end of a life. But while I was writing this story, I felt as if my life were just beginning. I have thought about the lost ones and their missed lives. I have tried to recapture faces, moments, familiar sounds—even the smells—of the fifty men, all sergeants, who passed through our Nissen hut on that muddy field in East Anglia. Most of them were killed or became prisoners of war. Out of all those men, only five of us survived at the end, and only two without any injuries at all.

I've been doing a lot of thinking and trying to recall dates and facts with the help of old papers I managed to keep. The group history, *Snetterton Falcons: The 96th Bomb Group in World War II* by Robert E. Doherty and Geoffrey D. Ward (Dallas: Taylor Publishing, 1989) has been tremendously helpful. The events that I have recalled here are true, but some dates may be wrong.

The Cold Blue Sky

I want to thank my editor, Fryar Calhoun, and my nephew Alan Novey for introducing us. An experienced writer and editor who also knows military history, Fryar made sense out of my rather jumbled manuscript, yet managed to preserve my own voice throughout the book. He also wrote the introduction to provide historical context for my story and prepared the book for publication.

My thanks to Marge Perin for taking my original notes and tapes and turning them into readable pages, and to journalist Jack Kneece, whose interest in my idea of writing my war memoirs stimulated me to sit down and do it. Geoff Ward, co-author of the unit history mentioned above and curator of the 96th Bomb Group Museum, was tremendously helpful in many ways, including furnishing photographs from the museum for reproduction in this book. I'm grateful to the U.S. Air Force Academy Library's Chief Photographic Archivist, Duane Reed, and to Lt. Col. David Hollenbaugh (ret.) for searching out wartime photos, including some of planes of my old 96th Bomb Group, from the U.S. Air Force Academy Library's collections. Thanks also to my old crewmate Charles Blumenfeld for making his wartime photos available, and to the author Peter M. Bowers for the use of an important photograph from his collection.

My family has been great. My mother and father, along with my sister Minnie and my brother Harry, sweated out my year in combat, and my thoughts were often of them. I'd like to thank my son Glen, whose careful reading, constructive criticism, and steady support helped this book a lot. Thanks to my daughter Jessica for believing her father could pull it off even at this late date. I am so grateful to Daniella, my loving wife of over forty years. She encouraged me to write this book even though talking about the war stirred up her own painful memories. The horror of her childhood in the Warsaw Ghetto and her years as a refugee make my own experiences pale in comparison.

I'm proud to have served with the wonderful guys of the Eighth Air Force, the 96th Bomb Group, and the 337th Bomb Squadron. It's been a great experience recreating it all in this book. Perhaps this was my twenty-sixth mission.

Jack Novey
San Francisco
November 1996

Fly-Boys of the Eighth

They've leatherbound sheepskin
On electrical clothes
While tethered to Life
By an oxygen hose
As cords that are countless
Guide heat through their suits
To gloves plugged in sockets
And prongs plugged to boots.

More cords for their gun switch
For flak they've steel vests.
And, God granting time,
There'll be chutes for their chests.
Just masks for their faces;
Cold phones for their ears;
But both God and Country
For their hopes and their fears.

—Robert Doherty

Introduction

by Fryar Calhoun

In May 1943 Sergeant Jack Novey, B-17 waist gunner, flew to England to take part in the air war against Adolf Hitler's "Fortress Europe." Across the Channel, the Germans held the European continent. In the East, deep inside the Soviet Union, Germany and its allies faced the Red Army on a two-thousand-mile-long front. Despite their enormous losses at Stalingrad, the Germans were preparing to resume the offensive.

The Western Allies still fought the Germans on the periphery of Europe. In the Atlantic, German U-boats attacked the Allies' convoys and tried to evade their navies. Allied ground troops were completing their victory over the German and Italian armies in North Africa which Rommel had commanded until February 1943. The soldiers who would invade France were beginning to gather in the British Isles—American, British, Canadian, French, and Polish. But the date of the invasion had not been set.

The British and American high commands had different views about the war. They agreed that the battle had to be brought to the German homeland—both for the long-term purpose of destroying German war capacity and for the short-run objective of relieving pressure on the Soviet Union. If the Western Allies were not ready to open a second front on the ground, they could do so in the air. But they disagreed on how and when.

The Americans wanted to attack Germany with ground forces at the earliest possible date and by the shortest route—across the Channel and through northern France and the Low Countries. The British, however, were short of manpower and burdened by memories of the terrible cost of fighting in France in the First

World War. They wanted to put off the invasion until fighting on other fronts had weakened the German Army.

The all-out bomber offensive against Germany served as a compromise solution to this impasse. (As for the invasion, that question was also eventually decided by compromise: D-Day would take place, but not until 1944.) Both British Prime Minister Winston Churchill and U.S. President Franklin Roosevelt were advocates of a bombing campaign against Germany. Some air commanders thought it would break the morale of the enemy civilian population; others emphasized the damage it would do to the German economy and weapons production. Still others saw it as a battle for air supremacy over the continent in preparation for the invasion.

After some bitter early experiences, the British bombed exclusively at night. The Americans believed in daylight bombing. Once they were present in significant numbers, the bombing went on round the clock. It was an exceptionally hazardous form of warfare, and one that grew increasingly costly to both sides.

In this memoir of the European air war, Jack Novey describes his experiences freshly and frankly, as seen through the eyes of the eighteen-year-old volunteer he was then, not the seventy-year-old veteran who wrote it. His narrative combines vivid moments of life-and-death combat with personal memories of friends and fellow airmen—most of whom did not survive. He recalls the events and the emotions, the sights, sounds, and even the smells of those desperate days and nights long ago. Like so many combat veterans, he confirms an old military truth: In the final analysis, soldiers fight not for God, country, or home, but for their comrades-in-arms—for each other.

★　　★　　★

When Jack Novey and the crew of the *Black Hawk* arrived, the Americans had been in the European air war less than a year. The British were old hands. The Royal Air Force had been locked in combat with the Luftwaffe since the summer of 1940, when the Germans conquered France and prepared to invade England.

Early in the war, the Germans used terror bombing against defenseless cities—like Warsaw and Rotterdam—whose national governments could not strike back. But the British were a different matter. Churchill, in office as Prime Minister less than a week, ordered the R.A.F. to retaliate for the Luftwaffe's destruction of Rotterdam on May 15, 1940. The air war was on.

At first both the Germans and the British restricted their bombing to military targets such as docks, railyards, arms factories, and airfields, although lack of precision made civilian casualties and damage inevitable. The Luftwaffe came dangerously close to achieving air superiority in the Battle of Britain. But the R.A.F. fighter forces held off the German attackers, and Hitler canceled the invasion.

In late August 1940, a Luftwaffe crew bombed residential East London by mistake. By Churchill's direct order, the R.A.F. responded by bombing Berlin (not very effectively). On September 4 Hitler, in a ferocious speech to a roaring crowd in the Berlin Sports Palace, declared unrestricted aerial warfare and threatened to destroy British cities from the air. From then on both sides cast aside all restraints. An R.A.F. attack on Munich in November 1940 was followed by the Luftwaffe's devastating bombing of the cathedral city of Coventry. The next month the R.A.F. raided Mannheim but largely missed the city.

At this early stage of the war, the German bombers carried a bigger bomb load than the British, and the Luftwaffe held the upper hand during the "Blitz" of the winter of 1940-41 and throughout the following year. Civilians and residential areas became the targets—especially the working-class neighborhoods that often surrounded important industrial complexes. Large sections of London and many other cities burned under German bombardment. The Luftwaffe killed 21,000 British residents in the first six months of the air war.

Meanwhile, the R.A.F.'s bombers had trouble finding their targets. In 1941 the number of British airmen killed trying to drop bombs on German cities exceeded the number of German civilians killed by those bombs. British fighters lacked the range to escort bombers as far as Germany. With no protection against German fighters other than their own medium-caliber machine guns, the bombers were easy prey in daylight. So R.A.F. Bomber Command turned exclusively to night raids. At night it was much more difficult for the German fighters to find the bombers.

Any initial British resolve to limit bombing to military targets disappeared in face of the fact that nighttime precision bombing was impossible. Finding the right city was difficult enough; hitting a specific target was out of the question unless the whole area was destroyed. Lacking any other means of coming to grips with the enemy on the European continent, the British turned to "area bombing," which could only lead to massive damage and many civilian deaths.

Gradually, British bombing became more effective. Navigation improved with the development of primitive radar. Specialized "Pathfinder" squadrons were organized to guide the bomber fleets to their targets. Bigger, more powerful, higher-flying, more heavily-armed bombers—particularly the Lancaster—went into action.

As a result of R.A.F. attacks in the spring of 1942, vulnerable German cities like Lübeck and Rostock, built largely in wood and dating back to the Middle Ages, were burned to the ground. The Luftwaffe struck back at historic English towns like Canterbury, Bath, and York. The R.A.F. then incinerated the center of Cologne, although the cathedral survived. Each side was trying to break the morale of the enemy civilian population, and in spite of the damage and loss of life, neither appeared to be succeeding. If "London can take it," as the popular slogan went, so could the Germans.

★   ★   ★

On August 17, 1942, the U.S. Eighth Air Force, flying from England, entered the battle with a modest twelve-plane attack, heavily escorted by British Spitfires, on railyards in the northern French city of Rouen. The Americans had their own strategy and their own heavy bombers—especially the B-17 "Flying Fortress," bristling with machine guns and designed to protect itself from enemy fighters without benefit of friendly escort. Self-defense would be necessary: The Americans intended to bomb during the daytime, yet like the British they lacked fighters with sufficient range to accompany bombers beyond the German border. Unlike the British, they didn't set out to lay carpets of bombs on cities. Equipped with the secret new Norden bombsight, American bombers would attempt to carry out precision daylight strikes on military and industrial targets.

At first the heavy bombers of the Eighth Air Force were limited to targets in France and the Low Countries within fighter escort range. It was not until the late spring of 1943, around the time Jack Novey and the crew of the *Black Hawk* arrived in England, that the Eighth Air Force assembled enough heavy bombers and crews for its commanders to try out the strategy of venturing beyond fighter cover to hit targets in Germany.

In the air battles that followed, Luftwaffe fighters and anti-aircraft guns took a heavy toll of the American bombers. Some of the bombers managed to hit their targets, although post-strike reconnaissance showed that even with the new bombsight, most bombs fell wide of the mark. Clouds often obscured the targets; later in the war, American bombardiers were instructed to bomb by radar —which meant that any precision was impossible. The inevitable result was widespread damage to non-military areas and heavy loss of civilian lives.

For the attackers, the cost in lost planes and air crews was also very high. During the summer and fall of 1943, when the *Black Hawk* crew flew most of their missions, the Eighth Air Force lost an average of thirty percent of its bomber crews every month—killed, wounded, missing, or shot down and taken prisoner. Only about one in seven crews made it through the twenty-five missions required to complete a tour. For an Allied soldier there was no more dangerous duty in the war.

The *Black Hawk* flew some of the biggest and most controversial missions of the air war up to that time. In late July 1943, on one of Jack Novey's early missions, his squadron searched for military targets around the great port of Hamburg, which was still burning from the firestorm set by British incendiary bombs on the previous nights. The firestorm destroyed eighty percent of the city's buildings and killed more than 40,000 civilians.

In August his wing made a "diversionary" raid on the Messerschmitt aircraft factory in Regensburg while most of the Eighth Air Force bombers attacked crucial ball-bearing plants in Schweinfurt. Bomb damage reduced German ball-bearing production dramatically for a while, but the lack of follow-up raids allowed the Germans to rebuild the factories. In Regensburg, production of fighter aircraft was set back. But so many American bombers and crews were lost on the Schweinfurt-Regensburg missions that the Eighth Air Force called off deep penetration raids into Germany for more than a month.

While the Americans recovered from their losses and brought in replacement crews and planes, the Germans continued to strip the Eastern front of fighter squadrons and transfer them to the West, as they had done since the first of the year. The Red Army's air strength was growing due both to Soviet aircraft production in new factories east of the Ural Mountains and to the arrival of American airplanes supplied through Lend-Lease. Because of the Allied bombing, German aircraft production now emphasized fighters almost to the exclusion of bombers, which had been used effectively against the Red Army earlier in the war. All these factors, coupled with the concentration of the Luftwaffe's fighters in the West, ensured a crushing Soviet air superiority on the Eastern front. (By April 1944 the Luftwaffe had only 500 single-engine fighter planes to face over 13,000 Soviet aircraft in the East.)

The Eighth's return to Schweinfurt in October 1943, one of the dramatic centerpieces of Jack Novey's memoir, was close to a disaster. Sixty American bombers were lost, more than twice that number were badly damaged, and 600 airmen were killed, wounded, or missing. On the other side of the ledger, German ball-bearing production was significantly reduced—but only temporarily. Once again American bomber forces were hurt so grievously that they could not follow up with timely raids on other ball-bearing plants.

In December 1943 the Americans introduced the long-range fighter the Allies needed: an updated P-51 Mustang with a more powerful (British) engine. Equipped with reserve fuel "drop" tanks, the Mustang could fly beyond Berlin and back. American heavy bombers began to pound targets deep inside Germany.

Then, in the spring of 1944—after Jack Novey and his crewmates had finished their combat tours—the Eighth Air Force bombed targets such as key French railyards and bridges to prepare the way for the coming invasion, and also attacked crucial German aircraft factories and synthetic oil plants. Damaging or destroying these targets would create bottlenecks in German weapons production and ultimately deprive the German armed forces of mobility. Attacking them forced the Luftwaffe to come out and fight. The final battle for control of the air was under way.

As the spring wore on, Allied fighters drove the Luftwaffe from the skies. The Eighth Air Force continued to suffer heavy losses—twenty-five to thirty percent of the bombers and crews each month. But the Germans were unable to replace pilots and planes at the rate of the Americans. Before D-Day, June 6, 1944, the Allies achieved the vital air supremacy that the invasion needed to succeed. In spite of the belated appearance of a few German jet fighters, the Allies maintained control of the air throughout the final year of the war. By the last stage of the war in the spring of 1945, the bombing had brought the transportation systems and almost all forms of economic life in Germany to a halt and had reduced German cities to ruined hulks.

★　　★　　★

Toward the end of his memoir, Jack Novey reflects on the painful question of whether the Allied bombing campaign accomplished enough to be worth the cost on all sides.

Certainly the costs were heavy enough—for soldier and civilian alike. The British suffered 60,000 civilian deaths from German bombing. Some 500,000 to 600,000 German civilians died under the bombs of the Allies (including some Soviet bombardments toward the end of the war), and 800,000 were wounded. To those losses should be added the tens of thousands of civilians in France, Belgium, Holland, and Italy who were killed by bombing.

Including the Mediterranean theater as well as the Northern European theater of the war, more than 50,000 American airmen —half or more of them from the bomber crews—died in the European air war. The R.A.F. lost around 70,000 dead, with Bomber Command crews accounting for 55,000 of them. Deaths of Luftwaffe airmen on all fronts totaled nearly 140,000, with another 156,000 missing. In addition, on all sides many other airmen were wounded or captured, many more civilians were wounded, and vast damage was done to cities and towns, especially in Germany but also in Italy, France, and the Low Countries.

Military costs included the dedication of precious economic, industrial, and manpower resources to the air war instead of producing more landing craft for the invasion of northern Europe, more ammunition, more weapons, and—most important of all—more soldiers and officers for the Allied armies that would face the Germans during and after the invasion.

On the other hand, it is hard to imagine the Allied victory over Nazi Germany without a strategic bombing campaign. Left untouched, all the industries of German-occupied Europe would have been available to supply the needs of Hitler's armed forces. Allied bombing did enough damage to key industries that Hitler's Armaments Minister Albert Speer had to disperse production from large factories into small, scattered workshops and new underground installations. This allowed German weapons production to continue and even to increase throughout 1944, but at a much slower pace. In January 1945 Speer and other German cabinet ministers calculated that because of Allied bombing, in 1944 Germany had produced 35 percent fewer tanks, 31 percent fewer aircraft, and 42 percent fewer trucks than would have been possible without the attacks from the air. To put it another way, the bombers had prevented the Germans from deploying an additional 10,000 tanks against Allied soldiers.

The bombing campaign caused other distortions in the German war effort. Hitler's urge to retaliate led him to keep a considerable portion of German aircraft production concentrated on medium bombers for too long. The Luftwaffe found itself short of fighter planes—and, even more important, of well-trained pilots—in the decisive battles of spring 1944. Meanwhile, the Luftwaffe had no heavy bombers, and its bombing of British targets dwindled almost to the nuisance level. Bombing of the German synthetic oil industry left both the Luftwaffe and the German army critically short of fuel and almost immobile. The German V-1 and V-2 rocket attacks on England in 1944 and 1945 were unnerving and deadly, killing thousands of civilians. But they were so random that they had no military value (other than attracting waves of Allied bombers that were unable to do significant damage to the concrete launch sites).

Allied bombing also caused the Germans to divert more and more human and material resources into anti-aircraft units. Eventually a million men (and almost as many women) served in the flak batteries. They tended some 55,000 anti-aircraft guns, including three quarters of the German army's famous 88-millimeter cannon, which doubled as the war's most effective anti-tank gun. Because of the Allied bombing offensive, all these artillery pieces were unavailable to the ground forces and stood idle for the long periods between air raids. Because of the bombing, a million men manned the flak guns instead of serving elsewhere in the German armed forces.

The Cold Blue Sky

For the Allies there was little alternative to their bombing campaign against Germany. With the great invasion postponed, bombing was the only way the Western Allies could bring the war directly to the enemy's homeland, disrupt German war production, and relieve some of the pressure on the Soviet Union.

The bombing campaign gave a much-needed lift to morale on the Allied home fronts. At a time when the Nazis were still victorious in the West, it was proof to the British and American publics that their governments were waging war against the enemy. Knowing that formations of Allied planes were bombing Germany day and night also helped to sustain the peoples of occupied Europe in their hope that the war was not lost. The waves of planes passing overhead carried the encouraging message that their oppressors were feeling the wrath of the Western Allies.

Most important, on the military level, the bombing of crucial strategic targets forced the Luftwaffe to take to the air and fight a losing war of attrition, rather than save its planes and crews for the critical battle over the invasion beaches. Allied control of the air was indispensable to the success of D-Day, and it provided an essential basis for the eventual victory over Nazi Germany. Without the bombing campaign it would have been a longer war with a more doubtful outcome.

The Cold Blue Sky

Chapter One

I was a B-17 waist gunner in World War Two. I used the skills I learned in the U.S. Army Air Corps gunnery school, as well as what the doctor said was my superb eyesight and peripheral vision, to become adept at shooting down German fighter aircraft so that our bomber could get to the target and back.

It was deadly serious work. If I relaxed and missed a target, I put myself, my crewmates, and the whole formation in danger. This was 1943, the worst year of all for B-17 Flying Fortresses and their crews. I flew twenty-five missions—the number required to finish a tour of combat duty.

Early on, I decided that the odds were heavily against me. According to U.S. Eighth Air Force calculations, the average life expectancy of a B-17 and its crew was seven missions. I lived each day wondering how I had survived the week. I never allowed myself to contemplate the luxury of completing all twenty-five missions. In a strange way, I was less worried about my own fate than about how my mother would take the loss of her baby boy.

Yet in some miraculous fashion I survived. Perhaps it is because God wanted to save some of us to tell you about it—the ineffable horror, the daily, wrenching, pervasive fear.

As I look back, it is all like a very bad dream from so many years ago. I was eighteen then—a little Jewish kid from Chicago who did not believe in violence. I had grown up in a very sheltered way. I was keenly aware of the absurdity of war, and yet when I was in my teens, I was so patriotic that I used to stand and salute when I heard the Star Spangled Banner, even if it was being played on the radio and I was alone. Then the Japanese attacked Pearl Harbor, I enlisted, and a year or so later I found myself fighting for my life day after day in the skies over Europe.

The Cold Blue Sky

*   *   *

When I close my eyes, I can still see it and hear it. The time is 0300 hours on a cold, rainy morning in England in the fall of 1943. Our base is waking up to a mission. I lie in my bunk, listening to the rain. Other men are snoring. I'm waiting to hear footsteps outside on the wooden walkways that link the rest of the base to our Nissen huts—half-cylinders of corrugated tin squatting in a sea of mud. Before long the sergeant called the Charge of Quarters comes tromping down the walk, opening the doors of other huts, and shouting out names. Then he opens our door and calls the names of those scheduled to fly today.

We're all grumbling as we get up. We go to the bathroom, wash up, come back to our bunks, and get dressed. It's dark, cold, and raining. We're wondering who's going to live and who's going to die this day. But we don't wonder too long. What's the use?

We go to the mess hall for coffee and bread. There's not much else besides the eggs, which are powdered, runny, and greenish. Most of the crew members eat very little. Some smoke cigarettes with their coffee.

We climb into a truck and drive over to the briefing area. Navigators, pilots, and gunners meet in separate rooms. We're wondering where we'll go today, whether the plane will get off, and whether the weather will allow the mission to take place.

The briefing hut is light and warm, with a stove blazing in the corner. If we could smell each other, we would be stinking to high heaven from not bathing, from sweating, from being hot and then freezing cold and then hot again. But we can't smell each other, because we all smell the same.

Some crudities are going around among the crews. Men banter with each other, some lightly, some heavily. Others are lost in their own thoughts. There is no surge of fright in the room, just a bunch of sleepy-eyed guys.

The intelligence officer pulls aside the curtain hiding the map and reveals where the long red tape will take us this morning. Today's mission to Germany means seven or eight hours of flying. The briefing officer tells us to expect heavy flak and lots of fighter opposition. There are some British Spitfires to escort us to

2

the coast, but no American fighters are on the scene yet. He then dismisses us.

It's time to collect our gear. First we pick up our parachutes and check them out, then we go down to the armory for our guns and gun barrels. Each gunner takes two or three barrels, in case they burn out—as they often do in intense combat. We take as many .50-caliber ammo boxes as we can and still have the plane get off the ground.

Hefting duffels bulging with our flying clothes, we climb into the truck for the ride to the flight line and get dropped off at our plane, the *Black Hawk,* a B-17 Flying Fortress. We load our gear onto the plane, climb aboard, and wait for the green flare to go or the red flare to abort. Because we observe radio silence, everything has to be done visually. Sometimes an officer drives out in a jeep to give us further instructions or tell us that the take-off time has been delayed due to weather here or over the target.

We wait patiently, trying not to think about what we're going to do—and what we're not going to do. Crew members who smoke climb down and walk away from the aircraft; the stench of aviation gas reminds them not to light up too close to the plane. We're parked right next to a field of Brussels sprouts, and everybody relieves himself there at least once or twice during the morning. The first row of Brussels sprouts is the healthiest I've ever seen, about three times as tall as all the other rows. They must be nitrogen-loving plants.

Around us, life is going on as usual. Cows are wandering around the field. I can see a hay wagon pulled by two horses and driven by a farmer's daughter, a great big woman who is standing with one foot on the brake. Pretty soon we hear the chugging of the Norwich-London train coming along the railroad tracks, which run only ten yards from our parked plane.

Inside the train the lights are on. We can see people having tea in the dining car and men in business suits and tweed jackets reading their copies of the Times, all commuting to London for work or pleasure while we wait to go God-knows-where, perhaps never to come back. These people are going about their business as if we and the war don't even exist. I can't help wondering what they think when they look out of the train windows at us. They seem so unconcerned. Aren't they aware that we risk our lives for

The Cold Blue Sky

them every day? Aren't they curious about all those B-17s all over the place? Do they have any inkling whatsoever about what air combat is like? Do they care? That British reserve is maddening. Why can't they occasionally smile or give us the thumbs-up?

A jeep pulls up, and an officer says takeoff is in about fifteen minutes. We climb back into the plane and start to put on our heavy flying clothes. I already have on my quilted underwear, my dog tags, and my uniform of wool gabardine pants and shirt. My lucky pants are so stiff with filth that they could almost stand up next to my bunk. I take off my G.I. boots and put on my little blue flying booties, my blue flying suit, and my blue gloves—all electrically-heated—and plug them in. Over that I wear my zippered flying suit, which is kind of dandy, with long pockets holding the various items making up my escape kit: rations, a compass, money in case we're shot down, and passport photos of ourselves in case we're lucky enough to be picked up by the Underground. I climb into my lambskin-lined leather pants, pull the suspenders over my shoulders, and put on the matching jacket. On my hands I wear a pair of silk gloves, a pair of fur-lined gloves, a pair of heated gloves, and mittens on top. It makes you wonder how we gunners pulled the trigger.

Our guns are still stowed, tied down tight so they won't wobble loose. As a safety measure, we haven't yet loaded the ammunition into the guns. The ball turret gunner is sitting in the waist with us. The radio man is in his compartment just ahead, the tail gunner is in the back. The top turret gunner is standing behind the pilot and co-pilot. The navigator and bombardier are in their little plexiglass compartment in the nose.

Finally, the green flare brings our four big nine-cylinder, 1,200-horsepower Wright-Patterson engines coughing to life. The pilot pulls them through all the throttle positions, beginning with a hum and finishing with a full-throated roar that causes the entire plane to vibrate.

We get in line, and ten minutes later we're roaring down the runway. We hear the furious noise of the propellers and feel the rush of air through the waist windows, big rectangular openings in the side of the plane. In our bulky, layered flying outfits we don't sit for takeoff, we just hunch and hold on until we're airborne. We don't wear our parachutes because there's not enough room for us to move properly while we're in combat. There is no place for us to sit or stand comfortably, and the other waist gunner and I keep bumping into each other.

Once in the air, we go about checking our guns, making sure the ammunition is all laid out properly. If one round of a .50-caliber bullet sticks out a little too far or is too short, it jams the gun—a disaster in combat. This sort of malfunction, called a "short round," is fairly common. So we have to make sure that every bullet is in the belt correctly. We do all this wearing our thick layers of gloves and mittens.

Meanwhile, our plane is circling, waiting for the others in the squadron to catch up. We're flying lead in the squadron, so the other six planes are trying to tie onto us. At the same time, we're trying to tie onto the group, and the group is trying to tie onto the wing. We're flying in big circles as we gain altitude. We link up and head over The Wash, an uninhabited swampy area on the eastern coast of England, then out over the North Sea. We'll be flying across Holland into Germany.

On the intercom the navigator calls out, "We're at 10,000 feet. Time to put on your oxygen masks. Also, let's have a crew check." All the crew members report in, from tail gunner to bombardier. Then we do a gun check. The tail guns rattle off, "Boom-boom-boom!" The waist guns go "Vroom-vroom-vroom!" The radio hatch gunner starts off and the ball turret gunner follows, shaking the bottom of the plane with his twin .50s. The top twin .50 turret guns go off, making the top of the ship vibrate. Then the navigator and the bombardier let their guns go. Puffs of smoke emerge from more planes as other gunners test their weapons. Our ammunition includes tracers to guide our burst of fire and correct our aim. Of every five rounds, one is a tracer and one is a phosphorous shell designed to ignite when it hits a target. The rest are armor-piercing rounds.

We're climbing higher and higher. We'll be on oxygen from now until we get back over the English Channel, about six hours. To make sure our masks are working properly, we have to check the little black bulb at the bottom of the mask. The bulb fills with moisture from our breath, which freezes into ice. Every four or five minutes we have to squeeze the bulb and break up the ice. As we get up to altitudes of 23,000 to 30,000 feet, the air temperature is anywhere from thirty-five to fifty degrees below zero—not counting the chill of the wind, which whistles through our waist windows at 150 miles per hour and more. Freezing to death is a constant hazard at these altitudes.

When we reach the Dutch coast, our Spitfire escorts leave us, waggling their wings to wish us good luck. Now we become much more alert, scanning our fields of vision. The formations are tight. We see flak off in the distance; we try to avoid it but it comes up toward us anyway. So we watch, wait, and wonder, in fear and anticipation.

It's cold. It's the kind of cold that creeps into every pore on your body and freezes the sweat on your back. If you pull off your glove and touch the metal of the plane, it will take the flesh off your fingers. If you have to pee, the urine freezes before it hits the fuselage floor. In an attempt to protect our faces, we wear big black masks with holes cut out for eyes, nose, and mouth, but they're terribly uncomfortable. So are the flak vests they issue us. They're so bulky and stiff that it's hard to stand up straight when you wear one. So we put the flak vests on the floor below us, hoping they'll do some good if shrapnel or bullets hit the plane from below.

We fly on. My ears are assaulted by the roar of the four engines and their thirty-six exhaust pipes resonating through the B-17's aluminum fuselage. Cutting through the engine noise is the whistle of the icy wind. I'm very tired. This is the fourth day in a row that we've been up at 0300 hours and have flown a mission. I lean up against the window, and for a minute I fall asleep. Soon the howl of the wind and the roar of the engines are transformed into music. I'm back in Grant Park in Chicago. It's summertime, and I'm listening to Andre Kostelanetz giving a free concert. Viennese waltzes swirl through my head. Then I'm jolted awake by the pilot's voice over the intercom: "Fighters at six o'clock! Everybody be aware! Don't waste your ammunition!"

And so it begins again—the shooting, the excitement, the hyperalert state of combat. The fear is gone, the adrenaline is up. On the intercom my crewmates chatter constantly and frantically. I see flashes from cannons of attacking German fighters. Our thirteen machine guns thunder in reply. Back to back, we two waist gunners swing our guns up, down, and around, trying not to slip on the growing piles of empty shell casings at our feet. The acrid smell of the guns pours through my oxygen mask.

We are in the midst of heavy combat, yet in my mind's ear I am still hearing classical music—Mozart symphonies, Ravel's *Bolero*. Somehow, I have developed a defense mechanism which allows me to run music dreamlike through my head while I fight back. I must have learned to escape into this fantasy world to keep from going crazy with fear. Part of me is fighting like a tiger, firing one burst of .50-caliber slugs after another at enemy aircraft. Another part is hearing music through the cacophony assailing my ears. I have no time to think; I just react.

The shooting dies down for a moment. Then it starts up again. I look out the window at an incredible panorama of planes going down and parachutes blossoming in the sky. In a little while the pilot says, "Ten minutes to target." The bombardier takes over the controls, and flak appears in big black puffs. The *Black Hawk* tosses around as if it is riding a carpet of flak. Shrapnel rattles off our plane like hail on a tin roof. A hole appears in one wing as if by deadly magic. The only noises I hear are the anti-aircraft shells exploding and the throbbing roar of our engines. A plane can blow up fifty feet from me, and I can feel the heat from the explosion, but no sound from the blast penetrates the layers of noise that wrap around me.

Looking down, I can see the flashes of light from the German anti-aircraft cannons. They seem to be aimed straight at me, and I wonder in a vague and dreamy way why they are not hitting us. Each flash of light means that an 88-millimeter shell is on the way. I sometimes muse about seeing the flash from the shell that will rise up to kill me.

Our formation finally leaves the German coast and the enemy fighters behind. We head out over the North Sea and start to lose altitude on our approach to England. As we descend below 10,000 feet, I take my oxygen mask off and reach into my pocket for my frozen Milky Way bar.

On a mission we go from ten to fifteen hours after breakfast before we have another chance to eat—that is, if we are up to eating when we get back, if we aren't sick or wounded or just too tired. It is impossible to take any kind of rations on the mission. In the thin air of high altitude, thermoses explode and a sandwich

The Cold Blue Sky

freezes hard as a brick. We have no way of insulating anything against the cold. So we are issued candy bars—Milky Ways, mostly.

I chomp off a small piece of my frozen Milky Way bar and let it melt in my mouth. The taste of the caramel and chocolate is exquisite. I savor it slowly. As it melts in my mouth, the tension and fear slowly recede from my body and my mind.

To this day, I keep Milky Way bars in my refrigerator. Every time I bite into one, it recreates that same feeling. Perhaps it simply conjures up my delight that I am still alive.

Chapter Two

My parents, William "Bill" Novey and Goldie Ruben Novey, were immigrants from small villages in rural Russia. My father's family were leather workers. My father and my mother's brother fled to the United States around 1905 or 1906 to escape almost certain death as Jewish conscripts in the Russian Army. Both settled in Omaha, Nebraska, where they married and had children.

In 1929, when I was four, we left our quiet tree-lined street in Omaha for Chicago, where we joined my father's brother and my mother's brother. We moved to an apartment in the back of a restaurant my father had bought.

Next door to our restaurant was a large empty lot. One night my brother and I came home from the 1933 Chicago World's Fair, a long walk from the Lake, and saw the whole lot lit up with portable lamps. Police were digging all over. I saw a policeman carrying a paper-wrapped bundle. Curious, I asked him what he had. He said, "You really want to see, kid?" and I said, "Sure." He opened the package and showed us a head with one ear and two eyes staring back at us. That was all that was left on the skull. This was my first experience of life in our new Chicago neighborhood.

My father's restaurant served breakfast and lunch to workers from the huge Majestic factory, which produced radios and refrigerators. We were very busy. My father cooked, my mother and my sister Minne waited tables, and I helped wash the dishes. We had an extra waitress, Hilda, and our dishwasher Kelly slept in the basement. To help pay expenses, my brother Harry worked in a country store in Red Oak, Iowa. We stayed from 1929 to 1933. For a time the restaurant made a good living—until the Great Depression. The Majestic factory closed early in the Depression, and ninety percent of our customers were fired. Business went bad.

The Cold Blue Sky

The year I turned sixteen, 1940, we moved to the Humboldt Park area in northwest Chicago. It was a neighborhood of various ethnic groups: Jewish, Polish, Italian, and some German. Division Street, the main thoroughfare, was right around the corner from where we lived on Rockwell Street. Division Street had trolley tracks; the old wooden streetcars ran constantly back and forth from Humboldt Park through downtown to State Street. It took about half an hour to get downtown on the trolley car from our house. Both ends of the trolley were open, summer and winter, with a motorman in front and a conductor in back to collect the fares.

Down the street were stables housing horse-drawn vegetable wagons and bread wagons. There were delicatessens and hot dog stands, and in the summertime, vendors sold watermelon slices and iced drinks on the street. For a nickel you could buy a kosher hot dog loaded with relish and tomatoes and French fries on the side. A slice of watermelon cost only two cents. On our block, Polish butcher shops sold pork and displayed rabbits in the barrels in the springtime. But in those days we bought our eggs and chickens and cheese from kosher shops.

The whole neighborhood was very lively. People sat outside on stools and boxes. The groups didn't mix a lot, but there was not too much animosity. Most of the Jewish families were Orthodox and tried to observe the holidays and Shabbas. On Friday nights my mother would light the candles, and no electricity would be turned on in the house until the end of Shabbas at sunset on Saturday.

The Depression was still on, and life was hard for us. I worked, my brother worked, my sister worked. My dad had lost his business because of the Depression and became a peddler. I helped him for a time. He went from bar to bar selling neckties and condoms—rubbers, as we called them. He also bought a used Chevrolet truck, and we cruised the Chicago alleys with me (age thirteen) at the wheel and my father standing in the bed of the truck, calling, "Rags and old iron! Rags and old iron!" People would come out with rags, newspapers, and scraps of metal which we would buy and resell to nearby Rushikov's Junk Yard. My father tried everything so we wouldn't have to "go on relief." Sometimes the whole family took in as little as two or three dollars a day. But we always ate and managed to pay the rent.

My mother kept an extremely neat, clean house, but it wasn't easy because we had vermin. My job was to throw out the mice whenever they were trapped, and my mother was constantly turning over the bedding, forcing the bedbugs out, and burning them with wooden matches.

We lived in an apartment house with three entrances. There were three floors and about fifteen one-bedroom apartments in the building. We all slept and lived in one apartment with each other. There was a back balcony and an alley to the right. In those days it was safe to play baseball on the street and, in the summertime, kickball. Chicago was hot in the summer and cold in the winter.

I worked where my brother worked, at the Abnate Coffee Company down by Navy Pier off Grand Avenue. Raw coffee beans were brought in green bags, roasted, and sold to various state institutions and private labels. The coffee beans smelled delicious, but the work itself was hard. I would hustle bags of green coffee that weighed more than I did and take part in the shipping and canning process. I got to work at 7:00 in the morning and quit at 7:00 at night. I was making about nine bucks a week at that time. My brother, who was five years older, was making fifteen dollars. And my dad even worked there part-time. But after he suffered his heart attack, working was difficult for him.

I had my friends Dave and Danny to have fun with. In the summer we'd go to Humboldt Park and look for girls. Humboldt Park at that time was a marvelous place. There was a lagoon and a big boat house, and in the summertime a big area in front was hung with lanterns. There were dances where recordings of the Big Bands were played, and we'd go watch the girls dance. You could walk in the park at 2:00 a.m. and not worry about it. We were on the streets all the time. There was no such thing at that time as dope. We had liquor in the house, but I had no inclination to drink. People smoked a lot of cigarettes. They walked a lot. They talked a lot.

My grandmother didn't speak a word of English, only Yiddish and Russian. She lived with her son—my Uncle Arthur—and his family. She would sit out front in good weather on a wooden box and watch the young Jewish people walk by in skimpy clothes, smoking and talking boisterously, and she would comment on their lack of morals. She would curse, "A klug off Columbus!" Translated, that meant "A curse on Columbus"—for discovering America and leading to the lack of Jewish morals in young people!

I had a friend named Harry Liebowitz, a handsome guy who was only in his forties but couldn't work because of a heart attack. His wife Mary supported the family. At that time there wasn't any kind of disability compensation from the government. There was no welfare. There was nothing except relief—the dole—and that was out of the question. Someone had to bring in the money. Either you got it from the family or somebody worked, because there were no charities that took care of you. You found ways or you starved.

My friend Harry would sit out on a box in the summertime turning dark brown, and we would talk about nothing in particular. I had no plans or thoughts of any future. Life was an everyday fight. I had quit school the fall semester of 1940 and worked at various jobs, ending up at the coffee factory. In my spare time I'd go to the library and read everything in sight. I especially loved Richard Halliburton's books, but I also read encyclopedias and anything else I could lay my hands on. And I read the newspapers. For a young man I was up on current affairs, and I talked constantly with Harry about the rise of Hitler and about the war which I knew for sure was coming to us.

The draft had already been put into effect. My brother was given a choice to volunteer for one year or be drafted, since he had a low number. The draft board told him if he volunteered, his service would be over in a year and then he would be out of it. Well, he volunteered for 1941, his year of service, left his job, and marched off to the Coast Artillery in the State of Washington. Little did he know that his one-year tour of duty would stretch to five years.

I left my job at the coffee factory and went to work at a garment factory where my job was relatively easy and paid twelve dollars a week. I worked on a manually-operated button machine stamping out buttons and buttonholes. There were about four or five of us males sitting there; the women did all the sewing. I sat next to an old man who spoke with a heavy German accent. It was summertime and extremely hot. The man would sit there without a shirt on, as most of us did. I'd look over at him and saw he was constantly crying. He didn't talk much.

So one day I asked him, "Why do you cry all the time?" And in a heavy German accent, he said, "Look at my stomach." There were wounds going up from the belt line all the way up across his chest. There must have been fifteen bullet holes. He said, "I vas a German soldier in Vorld Var One and I fought in ze trenches. I have got ze Iron Cross." He said, "I vas alvays a good German. I am a good German. Because I am a Jew, I vas kicked out. I am here now, vorking. I vas a business man. I had ze Iron Cross and I fought in ze var. I'm here now." This was my first closc-up glimpsc of what was happening to the Jews in Germany, aside from what I read in the newspapers.

I was seventeen years old but stood only about five feet seven and weighed under 120 pounds. I was wiry. My arms were skinny; I had pretty good forearms, but from the elbow up they looked like pipe stems. Under my shirt, even in the summertime, I wore about five or six T-shirts to give myself some bulk; otherwise, Frank Sinatra would have looked robust in comparison.

After my brother went into the service, the National Guard was activated, and the State of Illinois formed the Illinois Reserve, an outfit made up of young boys and old people. I joined and learned how to drill.

Then, out of the blue, Pearl Harbor was hit. I remember that fateful Sunday, listening to the radio, shocked, excited, and frightened by the news. I remember my mother and father looking at me, and so did my sister, who had just gotten married and was pregnant. We were all living in our little flat. I slept on the couch next to a small girl's crib.

About a month or two after Pearl Harbor, without telling anyone in the family, I went downtown to the recruiting office. I'd gotten the idea around the time of Pearl Harbor when I'd gone with my friend Dave to the Forest Preserves where we'd rented horses. I don't know how good they were—they were probably old, tired horses—but I thought they were fantastic.

So here I was two months later in the recruiting office in front of this grizzled old master sergeant who was still wearing a World War One uniform with the puttees, hash marks, stripes, and campaign hat. When I told him I wanted to enlist, he asked my age. I was seventeen, but I looked thirteen. Then he asked what I wanted to do in the services. I said, "I'd like to get into the cavalry." He looked at me, but he didn't laugh. He talked for about fifteen minutes. "At this time, there's only ceremonial cavalry. There aren't any fighting cavalry units. What do you know about horses?"

I told him I'd just learned how to ride. "Well," he said, "say you were experienced working with horses and you lived on a farm or on a ranch, for the first two years if I could get you in, you'd shovel shit. How does that sound to you?" After a moment he added, "Tell you what, if you want to get in, get your parents' permission." He handed me some papers and continued, "I'd try to join the Army Air Corps if I were you. There's all kinds of schools and opportunities for a young man." He gave me a friendly pat on the head and sent me off, probably expecting never to see me again. But this man and his advice changed my life and my opinion about myself.

One of our neighbors was visiting when I arrived home: Kay Arman, the daughter of a world-champion wrestler. Her brother also wrestled, under the name of Bobby Managoff. Kay Arman was a great big woman with a gorgeous voice. She went to New York and became a popular singer with a radio program of her own. Kay and her family were Armenians from Turkey. Kay spoke a beautiful Yiddish and was able to talk to my grandmother and my parents.

When I showed the permission papers to my mother, she became hysterical and shouted, "Never! Never! Never!" My mother was one of the most beautiful women who ever lived. She never complained and would do anything for her children. Despite the fact that when I was growing up, she could hardly speak or read English, she was the most modern-thinking person I have ever met in my life. And my dad was the sweetest guy. I was very fortunate to have these two great parents.

But I wanted to join up. Kay looked at my mother and said, "Look at this skinny kid! He's in and out of the doctor's office, he can't shit right, he's constipated, you can see the bones, who's gonna take him? Sign! Nobody's gonna take him." So my mother signed.

The next day, I went for a physical and to my surprise, I passed it. My mother went into shock when I broke the news. She couldn't believe it, especially when I told her I was scheduled to go to Jefferson Barracks, Missouri in three days. She must have felt she was losing all her children. I had another brother who died before I was born from a fractured skull suffered when he fell down the stairs. Her other son was in the Army, her daughter was pregnant, and now her baby was going into the service!

★　★　★

The day I went into the Army, I set off down the street with my mother trailing behind. I was embarrassed and sad at the same time, but I sure didn't want her to keep following me. I had tried to say goodbye at home, but she followed me to the streetcar, where she stood waving at me with tears running down her cheeks. I fought back my own tears. Seeing her like this broke my heart. I was also nervous and scared, wondering if I was doing the right thing.

I got off the streetcar at the induction station, which was near the Abnate Coffee Company where I used to work. There were a bunch of guys there, mostly from Chicago, some from the little towns surrounding the city. We were sworn in and told that now we were in the Army even though we still wore our civilian clothes. Then we were marched to the Illinois Central Northwestern Station to board a train for Jefferson Barracks, Missouri, where there was a great big training center for inductees.

We boarded the train, an old one, at about 11:00 in the morning. We immediately opened the windows, because it was a hot, stifling, humid Chicago day. The train started to move out of the station and through the nearby stockyards. Suddenly, it stopped in the middle of the stockyards. The stink of the cows, pigs, and goats was everywhere. The stench made eating our packed sandwiches a chore. There we sat for about four or five hours.

We arrived in St. Louis around 11:00 that night and were let off right at the Army base in a ravine. In spite of the late hour, the air temperature was about 103 degrees and the humidity close to 100 percent. We were still in civilian clothes which, after that long ride, were thoroughly soiled with soot from the train's smokestack. Tired and dirty, we were marched with our luggage up a road that led up the ravine. At a big warehouse we were issued barracks bags, some bedding, and a summer-weight uniform with shoes and underwear. Then they marched us off to our barracks.

By that time it was about 2:00 a.m., and we slept like logs. I got my first taste of what was in store for me in the service when, two hours later, I was rudely awakened to start the day. Outside, we lined up the best we could, a bunch of guys who never walked in a straight line before. Then we marched to breakfast. After breakfast we were taken to a big field where we stood around waiting, about ninety of us. Dump trucks started coming, dumping loads of rock and gravel and dirt all over the field. Each of us was handed a shovel and a rake and told to level all this and make a smooth field.

That was when the first thoughts of going A.W.O.L. occurred to me. Except for the stiff penalties, and the fact that they said they'd shoot us if they caught us (which I firmly believed), I think I would have gone over the hill. I was mad and muttered under my breath, "What the hell am I doing here? I volunteered for this?"

At noon we broke for lunch. I had already been served one meal in the service, breakfast that morning, when I had eaten only eggs. I didn't take any of the bacon or the ham because I'd never eaten that stuff before, and I was reluctant to break the habits of a kosher upbringing. But at lunch, all they had was pork and beans. So I said, "Well, what the hell." I was starving to death. So I dug into it and—Jesus—I loved it!

We were a grungy-looking lot, all dirty from the morning's work. We didn't even have fatigues on; we were wearing so-called "Class A" khaki uniforms. After lunch we returned to the field to continue the shoveling and worked until it was time for chow in the evening, a simple meal of meat and potatoes. Then we went back to the barracks and were allowed to shower, take off our clothes, do our laundry, and generally feel human again after such a long hard, day. But I admit I was taken aback by the group toilets that allowed no privacy at all. I was a sheltered little kid, and I was shocked. I probably wouldn't have volunteered if I'd known about the toilets.

We were being led around by a corporal, a little skinny guy from the Arkansas hills who showed his dislike for us city boys both verbally and sometimes physically—by stepping in our path, by tripping somebody, by laying on a heavy hand. None of us knew how to react to him and his bullying. He marched us out to the parade grounds where we stood at attention. We waited about half an hour and then out came a young man in his mid-twenties—younger than the corporal—dressed in custom-made khakis with creases you could cut bread on. He carried a swagger stick and wore the chevrons of a staff sergeant. He stood there looking at us. The corporal yelled, "Attention!" and introduced us to the head of our "squadron."

The sergeant didn't say anything for what seemed like ten minutes. Then in a polite voice he started to explain to us the facts of life: that we were in the Army and we were to do as we were told. He impressed on us that his word was final, that he was the law, and that we were his to do with as he wanted. At that point I felt more than ready to move on out of that barracks and on to the war.

We were marched to a large tent where, together with maybe two or three hundred more recruits, we sat on hard benches sweating in the heat while the sergeant read the Articles of War, the laws by which we were to be governed. To make sure that we stayed awake and listened, they had guys walking around keeping an eye on us. It reminded me of stories I had heard about churches where they go around and prod you with long rods to keep you awake so you have to listen to the sermon.

The first thing that impressed me about the Articles of War was that in the Army you are guilty until proven innocent. That bothered me, but there was nothing I could do about it. This went on for three days. We listened and listened and listened. We tried to keep awake. Mercifully, it finally came to an end. After that I was happy to get back on the drill ground—but not for long.

Drill consisted of marching in a group, in sequence and in step, making sharp turns together, saluting properly, learning how to present arms and snap to attention the way they wanted. The purpose of drilling was to teach us to observe discipline and to obey authority.

Once drill began, it didn't stop. We drilled for hours and hours. It was mind-numbing. If you made a mistake, the corporal found a big rock and put it in your right hand or left hand, whichever side had made the mistake. If you got caught chewing gum, the gum went out on your nose and stayed there until you could twitch it off (no hands). If you had K.P. duty at night, you worked all night, but it didn't excuse you from drill the next day. Every Saturday we went to the parade ground where the whole complement of Jefferson Barracks personnel paraded, 30,000 men. Other than that, we just drilled and drilled and drilled. Believe me, it was horrendous!

Below our barracks there was a school to train Army cooks. Naturally, their own food was far superior to what we were eating, and they would sell us apple pies and the like. That was one of the best things about Jefferson Barracks. One evening a farmer came by on his truck and dumped a whole truckload of watermelons on a part of the parade ground that was shaded by trees. We all ran to gorge ourselves on watermelon. We ate so much our stomachs were bursting. I felt like the juice was coming out of my ears, but it was a delicious treat after the physical hardship of the drill.

I made friends with Carl, a thirty-one-year-old Chicagoan. In the evenings when we had time, Carl, another guy named Brent, and I hung around together, listening to the jukebox at the enlisted men's club or telling lies about our love lives and our girlfriends. I had a beautiful Polish girlfriend back in Chicago, Natalie, an elevator operator at the Palmer House, a fancy hotel. I made up a whole bunch of stuff about Natalie for the guys. We'd go to the club and drink low-alcohol 3.2 beer, which was the only beer allowed to soldiers at that time.

One evening when we looked at the bulletin board to see what kind of activities were being offered, we saw a notice advertising a lecture, free coffee, and beer, and saying, "Please come! It will be very interesting and informative." Having nothing better to do, the three of us went. We were welcomed by an impressive staff sergeant in a beautifully-tailored uniform with wings on it. He sat us down and asked us how we were doing. We complained to him about how chicken-shit everything was, and he said, "Well, there's something you can do to get out of your predicament." We said, "What do you mean, there's something we can do?"

He proceeded to tell us about gunnery school. If we passed the qualifying test and went to gunnery school for five weeks of training, we would graduate as buck sergeants. Then I piped up, "I heard that gunners only have thirty seconds to live." He

Chapter Two

exploded, "Where did you hear that bullshit? The war hasn't been on long enough to prove anything like that! Where did you get that bullshit?"

I said, "I don't know, we hear it around here. That's why they try to get guys to volunteer. They try to make life miserable around here so you guys can recruit us!"

"That's all bullshit," he said. "Once you become a sergeant, you can go anywhere in the world." He told us how glamorous it would be and how we'd get out of this chicken-shit situation.

So I said, "Well, what do you have to do to sign up?" He answered, "In the morning, at roll call, raise your hand and ask permission to speak to the sergeant. He'll give you permission. Tell him you want to volunteer for gunnery school, and he'll march you over to the office and make arrangements to set up your physical and mental tests." "That sounds good," I said.

The next morning at roll call, Carl, Brent and I did as he said. Our sergeant looked at us and said, "Okay. Wait down at the office for me." When he finally met us there he said, "You're sure this is what you want to do?" "Yes sir," I said. I would have done anything to get out of all that drilling and our chickenshit situation. We stood at attention while he looked at us. Then he wrote a note and sent us down to headquarters. They did all kinds of testing there to determine recruits' intelligence, skills, and aptitudes and where they should be sent after recruiting camp: gunnery schools, weather schools, armor schools, radio schools, cooking schools, and so on—wherever the Army thought they could be best used.

We took the mental and ability tests first. They were the same as pilot tests, measuring our depth perception, hearing, and alertness. These tests were different from anything I had ever experienced. They were followed by a written examination which wasn't too difficult. The tests took all day long. I was shocked to come out with flying colors. My depth perception was extraordinary and the extent of my peripheral vision testing was such that I found out that by looking straight ahead, I could almost see my ears! This proved to be valuable because in combat I was able to see things clearly from all angles, and with a great deal of depth. Later, on the *Black Hawk*, I was the lookout who had the crew's only pair of binoculars.

19

The Cold Blue Sky

All of us who were applying for gunnery school were told to report for our physical the next day. I stripped down, and the doctors examined every part of me. Then I found myself seated before an eye-ear-nose guy. He was bent over, looking in my ears, looking in my mouth and prying my nose open. After looking up my nose, he sighed and said, "Well, young man, I'm afraid I'm going to have to disqualify you."

I asked, "Why?" He replied, "You have a deviated septum." When I told him I didn't know what that was, he explained that it was an obstruction in my nose. "It's most likely you're going to be flying at high altitudes and wearing an oxygen mask, so with the deviation that you have, you won't be able to breathe," he said. "That's it."

"That's it? There's nothing I can do about it?" I was stunned and almost started crying with disappointment. Then he said he could send me to the hospital and have it fixed. When I asked him whether it would hurt, he told me it was no worse than going to the dentist. I knew I could handle that. Then he corrected himself. "It's easier than going to the dentist. They give you a shot and you're out of there the next day." So I told him to set it up.

When I was admitted to the hospital, another patient was lying in a bed across the aisle. His whole face was purple, and his head and nose were so swollen that his eyes were just peeking through. I said to the guy next to me, "Jesus Christ, he looks like he fell from a ten-story building! What the hell happened to him?" Ever so casually, the man answered, "Oh, he was operated on for a deviated septum." I wanted to get up and walk out. I didn't know what to do.

While I was thinking this over, a nurse came in and gave me a shot. I started to relax. The next thing I knew, it was morning, and I was being rolled over onto a cart and wheeled off somewhere. I was pretty well out of it. Then, all of a sudden, I was awake again, leaning back in this dentist's chair. Somebody was bending over me and swearing. It was a doctor, his white frock covered with blood, swearing to the nurses and holding my head back. He was saying, "They didn't give him enough! He's coming out of it! I'm not finished yet!" He kept on swearing, wielding this hammer and chisel and working away at my nose like it was a piece of rock. I passed out again.

The next thing I knew, I was lying in bed with a throat so sore I couldn't swallow. And it was hot in there, over 100 degrees. One of the civilian employees was a big, cheerful, kind Greek guy who would swab me with cold towels and wash my face and my neck. I couldn't drink anything or even swallow. I was so miserable, I thought I was going to die. I just lay there, blood seeping out of my nose. I didn't even know what day it was.

I looked down the hall and—my God!—there was my mother and the mother of my sister's husband, who had family in St. Louis. My mother had come down for a surprise visit, only to find that I was in the hospital. She walked right by me without knowing who I was. She just couldn't believe that this disfigured person was her son. Finally, she stopped somebody to ask where I was and he took her back to the bed and pointed at me. I saw she was trying to keep her composure. "My God!" she exclaimed. "What happened to you? What'd you do? What happened?"

I had always had bloody noses, so I said, "Mom, I decided to stop suffering from bloody noses and take advantage of the hospitals and services they provide in the Army. They operated on my nose. They took out a vein so I wouldn't have any more bloody noses. And it was free! Isn't that wonderful?"

Thank God she swallowed my story. I was already accomplished at hiding the truth to spare her undue worry. She stayed with me for a while, then she left because she had to go back to Chicago the next day. And that was the last I saw of my mother for almost two years.

I stayed in the hospital much longer than the one day I'd been promised. I was hemorrhaging, and I ended up being there almost three weeks. Finally, feeling terrible but anxious to be back in action, I got out and went back to duty and back to drilling. The men were in the middle of doing obstacle courses. In my condition it was difficult, but I managed to get through.

About a week after I got out of the hospital, I went back to be checked out again and ended up with the same nose and throat doctor. I sat down, and he started going through the whole examination again. He didn't say anything, and it was obvious he didn't remember me; he just kept looking at my throat and ears. Finally he looked into my nose and said, "Oh, son, I'm sorry." I said,

"What about, sir?" He said, "I'm going to have to disqualify you for a deviated septum."

I sat there stunned. "Doctor," I stammered, "I just got out of the hospital a week ago! You sent me there! I spent almost three weeks in the hospital!"

He looked shocked. "Well, let me take a look again." So he looked and said, "Well, there's a lot of blood crusted in here." He scraped the blood crust away, took another look, and said, "You still have a forty-five percent deviation, but seeing what you went through, okay, I'll let it go." And that was how I was cleared for gunnery school.

After this ordeal, I ended up going to gunnery school by myself, without my friends Carl and Brent. Somewhere along the line, they either flunked out or decided not to go on, so I was alone. About a week later, I found myself at the train station with six or seven other guys holding travel orders for the air base in Las Vegas, Nevada. We were all pretty excited and looking forward to the trip. While we were standing around waiting for the train to leave, I saw a well-dressed little old lady staring at us. Then, to my puzzlement, she circled our group four or five times. Finally, she stopped in front of me and said in a loud voice, "Little boy, are you a soldier?"

It was hard to live that one down. One of the guys, Harry Brown, a saxophone player from New York, always greeted me, "Little boy, are you a soldier?"

Chapter Three

The train ride from St. Louis to Las Vegas took two days and nights. In 1942 Las Vegas was not what it is today. There were only two clubs on the strip, the Thunderbird and another one. The downtown area was very small. The town's principal supports were the big phosphate and magnesium plants on the outskirts, where a lot of people worked, and the air base, which at that time wasn't too big. Every training class was composed of 200 to 300 gunnery trainees, plus the base's regular personnel, who couldn't have numbered more than 300.

We started serious training the evening we arrived. They took us to what looked like a carnival penny arcade where we popped away at small moving targets with little B.B. guns and air rifles. With the help of our instructors, we started to learn how to lead the targets. Some of the gunners seemed to have been born with .22s and shotguns in their hands, and most of them were pretty proficient. Not me, though, not at first. I had never shot at anything in my whole life. But I found this part of my training very interesting.

In the following days, to get us used to handling weapons, we shot .22- and .30-caliber rifles and .45-caliber handguns using live ammunition. Then we shot skeet or clay pigeons flung into the air by a spring-loaded catapult. Afterwards, we climbed onto the back of a pickup and stood with our shotguns while the driver followed a half-circle course. Our targets, clay pigeons, flew unexpectedly into the air from six small box-like structures evenly spaced around the course. This was excellent training in how to lead a target—that is, how to guide the gun so that it would hit the target. To my surprise and joy, I managed to maintain a better score than the class average on these shoots.

The next stage was shooting .30-caliber machine guns at moving targets. After that we graduated to twin .50-calibers mounted on turrets on the backs of trucks. Little carts carrying targets ran by on tracks, and we banged away at them. That was quite a thrill, shooting these .50-calibers. They made a lot of noise, and it sounded like we were really getting into something.

A gun could be dangerous to the gunner as well as to his target. Someone neglected to fasten the back plate of one of the .50s, and when a soldier fired it, the back plate came off and smashed him in the face, breaking his jaw in thirty places. That was the first casualty of the war that I saw. I can still see it—the shocked expression on his face, his shattered jaw, the sudden quiet.

Then we learned how to shoot while flying. We hadn't even seen an airplane yet. At this time airplanes were still a rare sight. In my entire life I had rarely even heard the drone of a plane. A short time earlier at Jefferson Barracks, Missouri, a rumble of voices from the other barracks had gradually grown louder until 30,000 voices were yelling "Airplane! Airplane!" throughout the post. The cause of all that excitement was a little old plane flying across the base.

At the Las Vegas base one morning, we were told to report to the flight line. A sergeant pilot was assigned to each gunner, and each of us was given a flight jacket to wear. It was really hot on the ground, about 110 degrees, but we were going to fly at about 10,000 feet, where it was cooler. Each of us would go up in an AT-6 flown by those raunchy sergeant pilots and fire a .30-caliber machine gun mounted in the rear of the plane at a sleeve target being pulled by another airplane.

Each of us had bullets dipped in different colors of paint. Mine was blue. Our pilots were going to dive under or climb over the towed target while we banged away. I was trembling with excitement, thrilled to be training on a plane at last. We strapped in, and up we went, flying out above the desert.

My pilot made contact with the AT-6 which was pulling the target, then told me to unstrap my seat belt and stand up. I said, "Unstrap my seat belt?" "Yes," he commanded. I did as I was told, and we started to dive at the sleeve target. I tried to fire the gun. It was very difficult to keep my balance and fire straight. But I managed to fire off some rounds. Then we went into a steep dive, and I threw up everything I had in me. We went up and we made another half a dozen passes. Every time we finished a pass, I vomited again until I had nothing more to throw up. It felt like even my toenails were trying to come up.

When we landed, the pilot came over to me and said, "We can't allow that. You've got to get hold of yourself tomorrow. If you don't, we'll have to wash you out." Shamefaced, I followed the rest of the crew and him to where the big sleeve target had landed, not expecting to see any pieces of blue paint. Nobody was more surprised than I—except perhaps my pilot—to find that despite the vomiting, I had hit the damned thing pretty good. He looked at me and said, "Well, that wasn't too bad. See you in the morning."

The rest of that day, and many other days, were spent in ground school. Besides learning how to shoot while flying, we also had classroom instruction in aircraft identification, trigonometry, and accurate shooting. We studied weather so we could identify cloud types and figure out appropriate altitudes, and we learned Morse code, both sound and blinker. This kept us busy sixteen to eighteen hours a day.

The next morning I promised myself I wouldn't get sick again, but I did. I begged the pilot not to say anything and promised that I would get over it. The third time we went up, I managed to keep my cookies down and didn't get sick. But the following day I had another pilot and, much to my dismay, I threw up again. I told him this was the first time, and he didn't bother to check with the first pilot. In all we made about twelve flights over the state of Nevada, and I vomited onto most of it. But somehow I managed to maintain the class shooting average and when the six weeks were over, I was very proud to graduate. Of our original 250 men, only about seventy-five made it. We were issued our wings and commissioned as buck sergeants—"non-coms" (non-commissioned officers).

Were we excited that day! We went into town, where most of us hung out at the railroad station to watch the Los Angeles-Chicago train arrive, hoping to see a movie star. For me that was the high point of Las Vegas entertainment.

★   ★   ★

Back at the base, we awaited our orders. When they finally came, we were sent to a big replacement center near Salt Lake City, where we lay around the barracks waiting for our assignments. When I first went into the service, I was paid $30 a month as a private. Now as a buck sergeant drawing flight pay, I earned $128 a month. I felt very wealthy!

Salt Lake City was bedlam. There must have been a thousand Army Air Corps personnel from schools all over the country: pilots, co-pilots, bombardiers, gunners, armorers, weathermen, you name it, all waiting for assignment to training groups and posts all over the world. How we were chosen I wonder even to this day. Was there a group of men who tossed dice or picked names out of a hat at random?

One thing about being sergeants, we found out, was that we were no longer liable for K.P. duty or menial tasks. Not just any sergeant or lieutenant or captain could say, "Hey, soldier! Come on over here!" We were no longer subjected to that kind of bullshit. So for the first time I was able just to lie around and wait for duty.

At the Salt Lake City barracks, there was one guy who would come in every night at about 11:00, drunker than hell, and wake everyone up. He was loud and raucous, and all of us wanted to get back at him. Finally, a couple of guys rigged up a little gadget. He used to come in and turn on the light by his bunk with a pull-chain. They rigged up a condom and filled it with gallons of water until the damned thing was huge! They propped it up so that its weight was supported until he pulled the chain; then he would get soaked. When he came in that night, everybody heard him stumbling around and being very loud. He pulled the chain and, I swear to God, I thought he might drown. It was really funny. That cured him. He was mad as hell for a while, to our delight.

About thirty of us finally got orders to report to the Spokane Army Air Base in Washington. It was November 1942. The train ride from Salt Lake City to Spokane was spectacular. We stopped over in Boise, Idaho, and the mountains seemed to rise straight up just behind Main Street. I've never seen anything like that, before or since. Right outside of Spokane, as we were leaning out of the train window, a young lady with a camera took pictures of us soldiers and asked for our names and addresses. She took a shot of my friend and me and sent the picture to my home. I still have it to this day.

When I got to Spokane, I was assigned to the 412th Squadron of the 95th Bomb Group, which was just being formed. I also saw my first B-17 Flying Fortress bombers. They were very formidable and impressive. I thought, "My God, we're going to fly in those! I'm going to be a gunner in one of those things!"

Off we went at about 11:00 that first night, about fifteen of us crammed into the back of a B-17. We were told just to sit and feel how it was to fly. It was noisy, and even with the windows closed it was colder than hell. I looked around at these guys who were going to be part of my first crew, guys named Horvath and Harkey and Powell. I still have pictures of them today.

I was a little queasy bouncing around there in the back, but I was managing not to throw up. Then I looked over and saw Horvath sitting there with his mouth wide open like he was about to lose it himself. That was all I needed. I puked my guts out, saying to myself, "Well, there goes my career as a gunner." We finally got back down on the ground, and I told myself I really didn't like flying. But I kept these thoughts to myself, and I went up to Horvath and said, "If you hadn't started to throw up, I would have been all right." He said, "Throw up, hell! I wasn't going to throw up! I was just sleepy and yawning."

Our crew had our formal meeting with our pilot. I'll never forget my first pilot. He was impressive. He was in his late twenties and mustachioed. He looked like a darker Errol Flynn. What's more, he was a veteran of the Royal Canadian Air Force. He wore RCAF silver wings on one breast and U.S. Army Air Corps pilot wings on the other. We also met our co-pilot, who had maybe three hours of four-engine time. He was a roly-poly guy who looked a bit frightened of the pilot.

We were told we were going to train in Spokane for a couple of months—flying, learning how to use guns on the plane, making runs over the bombing ranges. The very next day we started to fly as a crew, and right after taking off we ran into a flight of ducks. They knocked out two engines and broke the cockpit glass, lacerating the co-pilot's face. We had to make an emergency landing and barely got back to base. Almost downed by ducks—what a first flight for a crew!

Flying was very difficult for me. I was violently sick four of every five times I went up. I was constantly worried about how I was going to make it. I tried to hide it from the crew. We were trying out various positions and learning who would be suited for what. At first I was assigned to the top turret. Swinging around from one side to the other, I could barely control things. Then I found that in the waist gun position, my stomach was a little less queasy, and I could always lean my head out of the window and throw up there without being seen.

I was still having doubts about whether flying was for me, but I kept it to myself. I was very depressed and didn't really know how to handle the situation. I was so reluctant to go up in the airplane from fear of throwing up that I would say, "Oh, our thermos bottle needs coffee," and then I'd take so long going to get the coffee that the pilot would take off without me. I was only able to do this once or twice until I was warned not to do it any more.

Then I got a break. We were sent up to an old Civilian Conservation Corps camp on Mount Spokane that the Army had taken over. We were to spend three weeks learning .50-caliber machine gun maintenance and other gunnery skills. Up in the pine forests it was cool and beautiful. I had never been to camp, but it was like what I imagined a boys' summer camp to be.

Our two weeks of training proved invaluable. It saved our lives many times. We sat at big tables and learned to assemble and disassemble machine guns blindfolded. Stripping a gun and putting it back together without looking became a matter of reflex. We learned to identify all kinds of gun malfunctions by looking at things like the stoppage of the bolt. We also studied fighter identification and did some more shooting with shotguns and .22s. It was a great experience.

One day we were taken to a building with a high-altitude pressure chamber. Instead of high pressure, it created low pressure; instead of compressing your body parts and fluid, it expanded them. The aim was to see how you and your body reacted. So in we went, four men at a time and a technician to operate and observe us. We were given oxygen masks and told how to use them. We could see the technician through the thick glass window. He talked to us via a loudspeaker in the chamber. Before I put on my oxygen mask, I noticed the technician looking at us with a weird grin on his face.

At a simulated 20,000 feet, he instructed one of us to take off his mask and for the man next to him to help if he could not get it back on. The first man, after thirty seconds, began clawing all of us. We got his mask on and he soon was normal. The next man reacted like a roaring drunk. The other man and I hung on until we were just about to pass out at ninety seconds. It seemed as if we were going into a pleasant sleep. The first two men were rejected as unfit to fly at high altitude. The other man and I passed with flying colors. Later, I understood the purpose of the test, but I thought it was handled dangerously.

After the training in the mountains was over, we went back to base in Spokane, then were transferred to a small air base by Moses Lake near Euphrates, Washington. There we were trained further, and we flew under adverse conditions which were said to simulate combat conditions.

This base turned out to be one big Army Air Force outhouse. It had no toilets and no electricity. It was late fall, cold, and snowing. The outhouses were so filthy, so encrusted with shit, that we made cardboard seat covers so we wouldn't come into contact with all the old crap. Everyone had his own individual cardboard toilet seat hung on a nail.

One night, coming back from the toilet, I fell into a deep, newly-dug ditch—no, not a latrine—that had not been there that morning. It extended four or five feet over my head, and the sides were sheer, wet, and slippery. It was dark, cold, and raining, and I was afraid I might die of exposure. It took me three hours of effort to get out of that ditch.

I remember going into the town of Wenatchee and seeing the huge Jonathan apples that they were selling there—apples big as pumpkins. I bought one, and it took me all day to eat the damned thing. One night some of the guys and I went to a dance. I met one of the musicians, who said his regular job was as a mortician. We got back to the base on time, but M.P.s had been sent out for all of us because some sort of alert was on. We learned later that this was the time of the Japanese invasion scare in California. We got into our planes and flew to Sacramento, California to await further orders, but we didn't have any ammunition, and our only bombs were practice bombs. Nothing more came of this.

The Cold Blue Sky

We flew back to Euphrates, then returned to Spokane for a month. For our final months of training we went to Rapid City, South Dakota for some very intensive gunnery practice over the Badlands. We arrived there toward the end of 1942.

I kept getting sick and tried to hide it. Because of this chronic problem I was having, the exhilaration I felt in flight training was tinged with misery. When the training was over in April 1943, we would be ready to leave for combat overseas.

About a week before we completed training, we were ordered to go to the dentist. Crew after crew lined up, and the dentist and his assistants made dental charts of us. Why? For identification. I remember kidding with this crew behind us and saying, "My God, can you imagine this being the only form of identification if we crashed?" This turned out to be an ominous comment. The very next day that same crew was on a training flight and flew smack into a mountain near Pueblo, Colorado because their altimeter hadn't been properly calibrated. The incident had a sobering effect on me. It was the first time I realized we weren't immortal.

One day down at the flight line, while I was waiting to take off, a squadron flight surgeon called me to the side. He looked at me soberly and said, "Sergeant, I'm afraid I'm going to have to take you off the crew. I think you're suffering from chronic airsickness. I want you to understand that flying at altitude, you'd be no good to yourself and no good to the crew because I don't see how you could function with an oxygen mask on." I protested to no avail. After he left, I went off and cried. About a week later the group left without me, and the base became a very quiet, lonely place. I felt like a coward and a quitter. I was really dissatisfied with myself and determined to get back on flight status.

There I was in this huge barracks all by myself. I went down to headquarters for orders and was put in charge of a detail of about twenty enlisted men responsible for cleaning up the air base—picking up cigarette butts and all kinds of menial make-work.

One day we were all sent down to Pierre, the capital of South Dakota, where there was a small air base. We flew down in a small plane and after we'd been there for a couple of days, we were roused one night by the smell of smoke. It seemed the whole prairie was on fire. We got blankets and shovels, climbed into a jeep, and headed for the fire. As far as you could see, the grasslands were ablaze. About fifty yards from the farmhouse where we pulled up were some burning fences and haystacks. We got to work and managed to beat the fire out around this area. There was no water, so we did it with shovels, blankets, dirt, sand, whatever we could find. Fortunately, we saved the farmhouse. Two days later it started to rain. By the end of the week, we were piling sandbags along the Missouri River outside of town, trying to keep Pierre from being flooded.

Back at Rapid City, the post was very quiet and lonely. I was obsessed by getting back onto flight duty. Then I had an idea. I went to the hospital and spoke to the head of the service—a colonel, a very nice, older gentleman—and gave him some cock-and-bull story that I had suffered from ulcers and stomach problems all my life. I asked to be checked out to see if I had an ulcer. I was admitted to the hospital for X-rays and barium tests. Naturally, they couldn't find anything wrong with me. So they automatically stamped me "Fit for Combat Duty" again.

Victorious, I went back and waited for a new outfit to come in. Later, I reflected that this delay in being authorized for flying combat duty may have saved my life. As it turned out, I ended up with one of the few bomber crews who flew all their missions and survived the war.

★   ★   ★

About a week after I was released for duty, a couple of replacement crews came through. The crew chief, a tech sergeant, introduced himself and brought me over to meet the rest of the crew. I met our pilot, First Lieutenant James Tolbert; our co-pilot, whose name I don't recall (he was replaced before long); and a fellow buck sergeant, Ray "Dutch" Eisenhower. I liked all of them immediately.

We started flying together, and I swore to myself that this time I would not get sick. I was up in the bombardier's compartment and had on a flight cap, similar to a baseball cap. And right away I got sick. But I didn't think anybody had seen me vomit into my cap, so I slipped to the bombardier's hatch, opened it up, and threw it out, swearing "Never again will I get sick!" I really made up my mind that I was not going to be washed out because of vomit, and thank God, it worked. Sure enough, I never again became airsick for the rest of the war. Nor have I at any time since.

It was really a thrill to be flying again, especially with such a fine pilot and crew. True, Lieutenant Tolbert seemed to be drunk most of the time, but he was a fantastic pilot, as he would prove over and over again. We trained for an additional two to three weeks. With my newfound freedom from the heaves, I actually started to enjoy flying.

It was early spring 1943, and we were in our final weeks of training, flying B-17s on bombing runs and gunnery missions. Our training missions were usually less than eventful—that is, until we met Mr. Bourland. Roused from sleep early one Sunday morning, we were instructed to meet at Operations at 0700 hours. There we noticed a tall civilian standing with our base commander. Our mission that cold morning was to fly this gentleman, Mr. Bourland, over his ranch, which was situated in a lovely valley on the approach to the huge cliff of Mount Rushmore. Mr. Bourland had a strong connection to the area: His father was the sculptor who created Rushmore, and Mr. Bourland was himself a sculptor commissioned to finish his father's work. We were to fly a low-altitude photo survey of Bourland's ranch and the monument.

The valley was about twenty minutes' flying time from our base at Rapid City. I went down into the plexiglass nose of the plane with Mr. Bourland. With the unobstructed view from the bombardier's compartment, that trip was heart-stopping. Our Flying Fortress was skimming along at tree-top level and lower. As we approached the entrance to the valley, we spotted an Indian woman who worked for Mr. Bourland directly in front of us. Hanging laundry on the clothesline, she looked up, saw us coming, and was so astounded that she fell into her laundry basket. The roar of our four engines in the narrow valley must have startled all the sightseers on the wooden viewing stands as well. Dead ahead were Washington, Jefferson, Lincoln, and Teddy Roosevelt. They grew huge. Then Tolbert banked the plane, missing Washington's nose by what seemed inches.

★   ★   ★

We finished our bombing and navigation training, flying at night to cities like Minneapolis and New Orleans for simulated bombing attacks. Then we received orders to fly to Salinas, Kansas to pick up the airplane we would take overseas. In Salinas my crewmate James Spell and I were peering into a jewelry store when the owner came out and said, "Let me show you something." I told him we didn't have any money or girlfriends. But he answered, "It's okay, I have nothing else to do." He ended up taking us home for dinner with his family.

Back at the Salinas air base, our co-pilot had gotten sick and was taken off the crew. A new co-pilot was assigned to us, Second Lieutenant Norman Macleod, who had just come out of the hospital. He and his engineer had survived a B-24 crash on takeoff from the Salinas base about two months earlier, at the very outset of their overseas flight.

By this time we were under orders that made us subject to combat zone regulations. We were not to communicate with anybody or tell them about our destination. We were all armed with .45s and .30-caliber rifles. We also had a Thompson submachine gun just like Elliot Ness and Al Capone. In addition, we had ammunition on board the plane. But the biggest secret was that we carried the Norden bombsight. This was supposed to be our ace in the hole in the strategic bombing we were going to do. The Norden bombsight was a top secret development. Data on air speed, wind speed, and drift were automatically fed into the sight, which was supposed to be capable of pinpoint accuracy. This machine was the key to the American strategy of precision daylight bombing.

Toward the end of April, we received orders to cross the Atlantic. Our flight was from Salinas, Kansas to Bangor, Maine, then on to Newfoundland, and from there to Prestwick, Scotland where we would await assignment. We were all very excited. At this time, my parents had no idea what I was doing or where I was going and I was wondering how I was going to handle the situation. They never knew until months later that I was in a combat situation.

Just before we reached Cincinnati, we ran into terrific turbulence and a very bad storm. We had no oxygen on this leg of the flight, so we had to stay at 10,000 feet and under. The plane was being tossed around like a ship at sea. All of our electrical equipment malfunctioned, putting us in a dangerous situation. We didn't know exactly where we were.

Our pilot, Lieutenant Tolbert, came down on the deck beneath the cloud cover, and we glimpsed an airport and the city of Cincinnati across the river. He brought us down at Lexington, Kentucky, on a very small airfield which wasn't really big enough for us. We overshot the runway. It was on a Sunday, and people were scrambling to get out of the way of this big B-17 careening toward them. We came up on the grass and stopped about five feet away from the fence. It was an exciting way to make contact with civilians, to say the least.

There was a National Guard unit at the Lexington air base, and their technicians were able to repair our radio equipment. It meant that our crew would have to stay overnight. We tossed coins to see who would have to guard the plane. Dutch Eisenhower and Russell Hubner lost the toss and stayed with the plane, while Vic Hunt and I went into Cincinnati, got ourselves a hotel room, and went looking for a place to eat. Hunt, a real ladies' man, split off to find some entertainment for himself. I was very shy and went back to my hotel room alone. I didn't know too much about how to find myself a lady for the night, so I went to bed.

At about two in the morning I woke to somebody pounding on the door. When I opened it, Hunt was standing there panting and clutching his shirt and shoes. He had his pants on and his jacket half on. He told me this wild story about picking up this lady and going home with her. All of a sudden he heard the door opening in the house. She screamed, "My God, get out of here! It's my husband!" Hunt grabbed his clothes, jumped out of the window and ran.

By the next day the plane was ready, and we had a rather precarious takeoff. After a day's flight we arrived at Bangor, Maine, where we were provisioned for our overseas flight the next day. I'd never seen anything like it. The whole air base seemed to be hacked out of immense woods, a cleared square in endless miles of green fir and pine trees. Today the name Bangor still conjures up for me the intense, fresh smell of the dense woods, the early spring chill in the air, the throngs of civilian personnel on the base, the pretty young women who gave us last-minute provisions, and the feeling of going off to a great unknown experience.

We took off the following day for Newfoundland. The flight from Bangor to Newfoundland was extremely interesting. I had never seen country like this icy landscape, which looked like it belonged on the moon. We made it to Newfoundland after about three or four hours of flying and waited there for weather clearance to fly on to Scotland. In a way I felt privileged, because in those days the only overseas flights other than the military were the Pan-Am Clippers and Flying Boats.

Bad weather kept us there for five days, during which we were among the hundreds of airmen quartered in an immense hangar. The ceiling looked about ten stories high. Our bunks were stacked five high. There was incredible bedlam inside that hangar. People were just hanging around, going crazy. Everybody was armed with carbines and .45s; some were even shooting out the lights in the ceiling. You could see guys waving money, playing cards and shooting dice. Others were betting on the most unusual sport I've ever seen: guys lighting their farts with matches. Whoever could produce the biggest flame was the winner. This was a real eye-opener for me. I'd never seen anybody behave like that before.

In spite of all this, flying was a serious business in Newfoundland. Infantry guards were posted on the perimeter of the runways because of concern about saboteurs landing from submarines. The planes were to be sent off in a certain order, and as weather conditions improved, some began to leave. We sat and waited our turn. By an hour or so after midnight, our plane was the only one left out on the runway. Dutch and I were guarding it. A jeep came up with our pilot, Lieutenant Tolbert—so damned drunk he could hardly walk. He had orders to taxi the plane to another area. As Tolbert climbed into the plane and started the engines, I whispered to Dutch, "I'm going to sit in the cockpit with him and if I give you the signal, pull that brake. I'll try to kill the engines."

Tolbert was in the cockpit and I was sitting next to him in the co-pilot's seat. Behind me was Dutch with his hand on the brake. Tolbert started the engines. Normally you start two just to taxi, but he started all four of them. I swear to God, I thought Tolbert was going to try to take off or crash into the woods. He revved up the engines, and finally we released the brakes. Tolbert taxied onto the runway strip leading to where all the other planes were parked about a mile and a half away. Then we were racing down the strip at about fifty or sixty miles an hour. Take-off was at ninety or ninety-five. I swore to myself that when the plane hit eighty, I would kill the engines and signal Dutch to hit the brakes. We got to the area where the other planes were parked—B-24s, B-17s, and some medium bombers. Tolbert slipped in between two other planes with about three feet of wing on each side to spare. He did a beautiful job. That did it. I wasn't going to doubt him any more, even if he was driving or taxiing or flying drunk.

Chapter Four

We waited nearly a week for passable flying weather. Late one afternoon we took off and flew over the barren Newfoundland landscape and out into the clear night of the North Atlantic. We were in a loose formation with a dozen other planes, all flying at staggered altitudes to avoid collisions. All of us manned our guns; we had been warned to watch for long-range German planes, JU-88s and Heinkels, that had shot down an occasional B-17. Our flight became more dangerous as we neared the British Isles, which were still being overflown by enemy aircraft.

So we were on alert for that entire cold, lonely flight. We stayed awake watching the stars. We were at 7,000 or 8,000 feet as dawn broke. Then we flew over some islands and land that may have been part of Ireland. Finally, the navigator said we were approaching the Scottish coast. We made landfall and set down at Prestwick Air Base, which was an indoctrination base for all the crews coming to England.

We released our plane, which was put under guard, and went to our quarters in the basement of an old castle which had been built in the thirteenth or fourteenth century. It was so wet in there that water was dripping off the walls, leaving the stone floor under an inch or two of water. Even the bedding was damp.

Soon after we arrived, we did a little exploring. We walked around the castle and down to the village, where we met a bunch of little boys with Scottish accents who kept asking for chewing gum. We thought they were cute, so everyone gave them gum and pennies.

The next day, after a miserably damp night trying to sleep, we took our plane to Burtonwood, a big Air Force modification center where U.S. planes were given final technical preparations for combat duty. There the crew left the plane and boarded a train for the city of Bedford. I remember standing in the railroad station outside Prestwick, waiting for the train and being issued our arms. We strapped on .45s while the British civilians looked at us as if we were from outer space. Carrying all our gear, we probably looked like it.

After a two-hour ride through lovely countryside, we arrived in Bedford, England, another indoctrination center where we spent two weeks. The first night, we were allowed some time off, and we went into a little village and walked around the green, which had a little stream running through it. I thought it was the most beautiful thing I'd ever seen.

There was a pretty young lady sitting with her mother. She smiled at me and said, "Hello, Yank." I stopped to chat with her. She was pretty, so I asked if I could take a walk with her. We climbed a hillside and sat down. There were cows walking around, coming up and brushing past us. For a city boy from Chicago this was really something.

As we lay on the grass talking, she told me she had a boyfriend. Then she joked that I looked brand new, which I was. I guess she was just being nice to me. As we were lying there, I heard a roar. All of a sudden a formation of Fortresses, twenty or thirty of them, flew over low and circled, ready to peel off and land. The throbbing sound and impressive sight of the planes bristling with guns sent my adrenaline soaring. With pride I told my young companion that I was going to be flying in one of those and fighting the war.

★   ★   ★

At the base in Bedford we went to a ground school staffed by a lot of R.A.F. instructors and a few American pilots and crew members. (I don't believe any crew had yet finished a tour of duty. This was before the *Memphis Belle* made its famous last flight on June 9, 1943.) Here they taught us all sorts of things, from English coinage to more fighter aircraft identification. We had to be able to identify enemy fighters as well as the British fighters which were going to be escorting us. There were only a few American fighters in England at the time, P-47s and P-38s, and we did not see them for months.

After two weeks we were taken by truck to a little village in East Anglia about an hour and a half away. Snetterton Heath was about eighty miles northeast of London and about thirty miles northeast of Cambridge. It was the base of the newly-arrived 96th Bomb Group. Among the first American bomber units to arrive, the 96th had been in Snetterton Heath for only a week. We were assigned to the 413th Bomb Squadron, whose first sergeant came out to show us to our quarters. He was a decent guy, especially compared to the sergeants we had known back in the States. He seemed to care about us as individuals.

The scene around us was a blend of air base, farmhouses, and cows grazing—all in all, a peaceful sight. The beautiful green countryside was quiet, and the air was wonderfully clean. It was late May, and England was on double daylight savings time. I remember that guys on the air base were playing baseball at 10:00 p.m.

On the way to our Nissen hut, the sergeant told us that we were the second replacement crew to get into the 96th and that we were taking the place of another crew that had been shot down. Inside the hut the other crews looked at us, but there were no fond hellos or fond anything. After all, we were replacing people —friends, probably—who'd been shot down. We put down our belongings and tried to make ourselves comfortable. One of the others came over and said, "Don't get too comfortable because most guys aren't here too long." I said, "What do you mean by that?" "People just don't hang around too long," was his retort. I didn't particularly appreciate what he was telling me.

Up to this time, I hadn't given much thought to what I was going to be doing. None of us had. Never once when I was in gunnery school or in B-17 flight training had I really thought about what I was training to do. It seemed to lie on the other side of an opaque curtain. Now that I was overseas, the thought would penetrate once in a while, and I would get a little scared. But I had no idea of the intense combat we were going to see.

No missions were scheduled for the next day, so we were briefed to take a practice flight. This was more necessary training for our group. We became a pretty good group under the command of Lieutenant Colonel Archie J. Old, Jr. The colonel was sold on training, training, and more training. During those first few weeks at Snetterton Heath we were either flying practice missions or doing ground training.

The first scheduled mission, we heard, had been a snafu. Planes were all over the sky. Few got to the rendezvous point, and a lot of bad things happened. In one incident that got my attention, a waist gunner's machine gun had accidentally gone off while it was still in its stowed position, pointed at the rear of the airplane. The burst of .50-caliber shells had wounded the tail gunner and shot out the controls of the B-17's horizontal stabilizer, so the plane was unable to land.

The pilot, Lieutenant Darrol Rogers, barely managed to keep the plane under control while the crew bailed out. But the tail gunner, Dominic Beneditto, had been shot twice in the groin. His left testicle was shot off. He was in such a helpless condition and was bleeding so badly that he wasn't able to pull the ripcord of his parachute. So they rigged up a guideline, threw him out of the airplane and held the guideline. Luckily his chute managed to open. Later, after he got out of the hospital, Rogers' wounded tail gunner Dominic joined our crew as my partner in the waist, replacing Russell Hubner, who went nuts.

Eventually the entire crew bailed out—except the pilot, Lieutenant Rogers, who took the crippled plane over The Wash, a desolate area on the coast which was used as a training area by the Allied air forces, and jettisoned its bombs, then headed out to sea. Unable to get out, he crashed and became the 96th Bomb Group's first fatality.

★   ★   ★

One day after a practice flight, we were put on alert for our first real mission the next day, July 4, 1943. Our crew was being temporarily spread out among more experienced crews so that we could get some combat experience before we went out on our own. The brass thought that was the best way to introduce new crews to the war. Along with our other waist gunner, Hubner, I was going to fly with the crew of a B-17 called *Kipling's Error*.

We went to sleep that night excited but apprehensive and were awakened at 0300 hours. At the mission briefing, my first, the big map had a red ribbon stretched from our air base in East Anglia southwest over England to the Cornish coast and out over the ocean to the Atlantic coast of western France. Our target was La Pallice, where the Germans had built a submarine base with underground and underwater bunkers for the U-boat fleet. Our bombers were to destroy their facilities and any submarines that happened to be there. It was a prime target. It would also be a long flight. To get there and back, we would be in the air for eleven hours.

Inside the plane, I started to install my gun, but my hands were shaking so much that the other waist gunner had to come over and help me. I remember that the host crew's radio man, Richard Hazelton, was particularly kind and helpful. He was several years older than most of us. Before takeoff, the navigator came around and checked our oxygen equipment to see that nothing was clogged in the tubes and that the little bubbles in our oxygen gauges were going up and down as we breathed.

About an hour after we boarded the plane, we took off and climbed in wide circles to about 9,000 feet, rendezvousing first with our squadron, then with our group. (A squadron had seven aircraft: two basic "combat elements" of three planes each, and the squadron leader. A group consisted of four squadrons.) When the group was together, we headed off to rendezvous with our wing. In all, 105 B-17's were on the way to La Pallice.

After we left the south coast of England near Plymouth and headed out over the North Atlantic, we test-fired our guns and made a big racket. We were up at oxygen level, which is 10,000 feet and higher, and it got colder and colder. I had never experienced any cold so intense. We were wearing our heated suits, but all they did was keep us from freezing to death. Nor had I ever flown this long at altitude. The mission seemed to take forever. The hours kept passing, and nothing happened.

Below, the Atlantic was gray and stormy, but up where we were the air was fairly smooth. We kept in close formation because long-distance JU-88s, capable of flying up to five and six hours, were said to be on patrol from bases in France. Except for the anxiety of waiting, I felt pretty good. I felt like a pioneer in a covered wagon going into dangerous territory, waiting for the Indians to strike at any moment. We proceeded along the coast and then approached the target area. The navigator said we were reaching our "I.P." (initial point), where we were to line up for the target.

The Cold Blue Sky

The colonel in charge radioed, "Everybody make a 180-degree turn." As soon as we turned, scattered flak bursts started appearing among the forward elements, gradually enveloping us. I could hear the "Wroof! Wroof!" of the shells exploding. Pieces of flak rattled off the plane.

Suddenly I saw a German fighter, a Messerschmitt ME-109, approaching our formation. Just one. Everybody opened fire on it. Streams of tracers marked the paths of our bullets. There must have been thousands of rounds of .50-caliber ammunition converging on that single plane. Finally, it blew up. The pilot must have been desperate, suicidal, or inexperienced. He didn't last long.

That was the one and only fighter attack we had to contend with. We bombed the target, turned back out to sea, and came home. So far the air war didn't seem too bad. Little did I know.

When we landed, we immediately went over to the debriefing room, which was filled with intelligence officers, one for each crew. We were seated at a large table and told to describe in detail everything we'd seen. We were pretty tired. We'd been up since 0300 hours, and it was now about 1700 hours—5:00 in the afternoon. So we got something to eat and went to bed.

★   ★   ★

On July 10 Hubner and I were once more assigned to fly the mission with the crew of *Kipling's Error*. Again we got up at 0300 hours. This time we went for breakfast first, then to the briefing room. When the map was uncovered, our target was Le Bourget Airfield north of Paris—the field where Lindbergh had landed after flying across the Atlantic in 1927. It was a strange sensation to be ordered to bomb a field with so much history. But now Le Bourget was a major repair depot and staging center for the Luftwaffe (German Air Force), and Luftwaffe installations were prime targets for our bombers.

We took off, got into formation, and were escorted by Spitfires to the French coast, which was about as far as they could go and still make it back. They were only short-range fighters and couldn't carry much fuel. The minute the Spitfires turned back, the sky was filled with German fighters, Goering's famous "yellow noses." These Messerschmitt 109s and Focke-Wulf 190s were the

42

best fighters in the world, flown by superbly trained veteran pilots. We were under constant air attack from the time we hit the French coast until we got to the target and back to the coast. But the cloud cover over the target was too heavy, so we never released our bombs.

As soon as we left the target area and the flak stopped, German fighter attacks began again. I saw enemy fighters twisting through our formation, trailing smoke and apparently out of control. Then, as they got close to our bombers, they straightened up, turned, and strafed our planes from one end to the other. I'd never seen anything so deadly clever in my life. The attacks were persistent and ruthless, and Fortresses kept going down in smoke and flames as we fought our way back to the French coast.

One B-17 in our group became a legend on this mission. *Wabbit Twacks,* piloted by Captain Walt Flagg, was hit and had to drop out of formation and fly low, "on the deck." I looked down to see what seemed to be dozens of German fighters circling Flagg's plane. I thought there was no way I would ever see Flagg's crew again. German fighters continued to attack the struggling bomber as it flew out over the Channel. But *Wabbit Twacks* made it home on two engines, shooting down nine enemy aircraft along the way—an Eighth Air Force record. The plane was riddled from nose to tail with bullet and flak holes, but the whole crew was unhurt. It was incredible.

Flagg and all his crew but one were awarded Silver Stars. The sole exception was our own crew's pilot, Lieutenant James Tolbert, who had served as Flagg's tail gunner on the mission. I thought Tolbert deserved some sort of medal just for folding his lanky frame into the tail gunner's bubble. He must have contributed to that B-17's survival and probably shot down some Germans. It seemed unjust for him not to get a medal, too.

On July 14 we flew our first mission as a crew. Once more we headed for Le Bourget. The experience we'd gained in our earlier flights paid off. At the controls, Lieutenant Tolbert flew a tight formation, everyone was alert, and our gunnery was accurate. It was another intense mission, with plenty of flak and fighter opposition. Some moments are burned into my memory.

I watched one of our planes burst into flames and drop out of formation. A waist gunner bailed out. His parachute snagged on the tail and, as the plane went into a dive, I could see both him and the parachute flapping behind like a weighted streamer. I couldn't hear the noise of the plane or the gunner's scream as, in slow motion, he fell to his death. It was macabre, like a silent horror movie.

Guns were pounding all around us. Our airplane had twelve or thirteen .50-caliber machine guns firing, sometimes in unison. The wind was howling through the waist windows. The engines were roaring. The shells piling up around my feet made the footing slippery, and I was having difficulty staying upright. Hubner, the other waist gunner, was similarly occupied. It was such an incredible, chaotic, desperate experience that I had no time to be scared.

Everywhere I looked, our bombers were being attacked, and here and there German planes were going down. Suddenly a German fighter overtook our plane on my side. He flew directly abreast of me, and I fired everything I had into him. He exploded.

Then we were on our bomb run toward Le Bourget, and the shooting stopped. Enemy fighters did not usually follow the bombers into the flak over the target area. We made a successful bomb run in medium to heavy flak. I think several of our planes were lost to flak that day. I could see Paris off to the right as we approached the target.

I was high during the fight and after. My juices were still flowing all the way back home. To this day I don't know of anything in life to equal that feeling. When we landed, the high was evident among all of us. The energy crackled. We had a lot of tension to let off after long hours of constant combat, of shots being fired at us and our buddies. We were all shoving each other around and congratulating ourselves. We had proven that we could work together as a good combat unit.

We walked over to the Red Cross truck where two girls were serving coffee, doughnuts, and Spam sandwiches. I grabbed a mug of hot chocolate and sat with my Spam sandwich. Nothing had ever tasted so good! I was so happy to be alive. Then we went on to the debriefing room. It was bedlam. The noise of excited conversations was almost deafening. But by now my tension was draining away, to be replaced by sheer exhaustion. I could hardly move. After debriefing we stowed our equipment, took our parachutes back to the parachute shack, and turned our guns over to the care of the armorers. I went to bed.

*   *   *

Three days later, at 0130 hours, I heard the clip-clop of the Charge of Quarters on the walkway. He was opening doors and shouting, "Up and at 'em! Up and at 'em!" He came to our hut and called the names of those who were flying.

I could hardly open my eyes. I went for coffee, then to the briefing room. This time we were going to Germany. Our target was Hamburg. I started to get frightened. It was raining, and the sky was black. How were we going to take off in that soup? A briefing officer said the weather over the Hamburg area would be maybe two- to three-quarters cover, with enough breaks for us to get in.

We were warned that the city would be heavily defended by fighters and flak. We were to come in over the Dutch coast, then fly out across the North Sea and into Hamburg, make a turn around the city, and come back over the North Sea again.

But the German fighters didn't make it easy. Lieutenant Eldridge Shelton's plane, *Sack Time,* was flying in formation just to our right. After we dropped our bombs, I was looking at his plane, and suddenly there was a black explosion. The big yellow emergency life raft came out of the side of Shelton's plane just behind the wing. The raft was tied to the plane with a nylon rope so that if the plane had to ditch, the raft would stay there until released. The raft inflated as it came out and wrapped itself around the horizontal stabilizer on the tail, locking it into a down position and causing the plane to go into a steep dive.

It looked as if somebody had tied a string to the plane and was yanking it. The plane disappeared right in front of my eyes, dropping from 26,000 feet down to 11,000 feet—an unimaginable 15,000-foot dive. I knew a couple of guys on the crew. They bunked next to us in the same hut and had arrived in England at about the same time we had. I never expected to see them again.

Back at the base, just after we landed, we watched a plane all covered in yellow roll down the runway and park next to us. Sure enough, it was Shelton's B-17. The violent banging of the raft against the tail had caused its yellow paint to flake off in tiny particles. The sides of the plane were completely covered in paint. The raft was gone, but we could see the big hole where it had come out, and the big yellow rope was still wrapped around the horizontal stabilizer.

As if that weren't enough, a moment before the pilot turned off the number two engine, the prop came off and smashed into the airplane right between the bombardier's nose and the cockpit. It tore a hell of a hole in the plane. In our unit history there's a picture of *Sack Time* with this huge hole and number two engine with a missing prop.

It was exciting when the crew finally came out; they looked like they had been painted yellow all over—especially the waist gunners. They looked like something out of a comic book. Not only did Shelton's crew survive this frightening mission, but they also lived through the entire war.

After this ordeal I was too exhausted to eat. I went to my hut, where the fire was out and everything was cold and damp, including the bedding. I crawled into bed and shivered myself to sleep, trying not to remember what I had just seen.

On July 28 we were sent to bomb the Focke-Wulf aircraft factory at Oschersleben, about 80 miles southwest of Berlin. Of our whole crew, only five were flying a mission that day. Hubner and I were together again, Bills was going on another plane, and our pilot Tolbert on yet another. After the briefing, I noticed there were more guys praying this morning than usual. The Catholic chaplain was busy with his blessings and comfort. The Protestant chaplain was walking among the men.

We got our gear together and climbed into the truck for the ride to the flight line. In the truck it was still dark. I heard a guy with a gorgeous tenor voice singing Irish songs in the back of the truck. I listened to him enthralled, but at the same time I felt sad. The guy next to me said, "You know who that is? That's Don Gordoni." Gordoni had played the original All-American boy, Jack Armstrong, on the radio and was as well known and popular as the stars of today's modern soap operas. Radio was even more popular then than television is today.

The guy beside me in the truck kidded me about listening to Jack Armstrong stories with their clean-cut heroics and Horatio Alger themes. And it was true. In our neighborhood all the kids listened faithfully to Jack Armstrong and cheered when he fought off the bullies. All of us had a mental image of Gordoni as big and blond, and he turned out to be this small, dark Italian boy with a great voice. That was the last I heard of Don Gordoni. He was killed in action that very day. Those were his last songs. To hear him sing at the back of the truck, then for him to die that day was too sad to express in words.

We took off in a blinding rain. All our planes were heavy with gasoline and the maximum bomb load, and we barely cleared the tree tops. I was scared. Our assigned bombing altitude was 27,000 feet, but just before takeoff the altitude was changed to 17,000 feet because of clouds at the higher altitude. We rendezvoused with our squadron, the rest of the group, and the wing, then headed out over the Channel, crossed Holland, flew across a corner of the North Sea, and headed into Germany.

Throughout this mission my fear never left me. I couldn't help wondering what we were doing there. I felt like a little boy lost in a vast snowy woods. Everything was so disorganized. The cloud cover was so thick that we had to spread apart for safety's sake. Now, squadrons were breaking up and individual planes were flying separately. The group ahead of us ran into scattered fighter opposition. Some of the fighters came on to attack our group. I caught occasional glimpses of the ground through holes in the clouds, but we had difficulty finding the target area. Finally, we gave up on Oschersleben and headed home on a route that took us over Hamburg. The wing commander radioed us to drop our bombs on any good target of opportunity.

The R.A.F. had bombed Hamburg two of the past three nights and had created a devastating firestorm. As we passed through a clear patch, I looked down and saw the great city shimmering through the heat waves. Fires glowed from one end of the city to the other. It was a shocking sight: destruction as far as the eye could see. Even at 17,000 feet the heat was so intense that my face was prickling as if I were standing in front of an open fireplace.

Behind us I saw a plane accidentally drop its load of bombs directly onto one just below. The lower B-17 was totally destroyed. In it was my friend Wilson Bills, the engineer from our crew who had just been notified that his wife was pregnant. Now the baby would never know its father. (I recently told this sad story to Bills' brother, who had put an ad in one of the Air Force magazines to see if anyone knew what had happened to his brother.)

As we were clearing the harbor, I saw a B-17 ditch right into the water and five or six German fighters follow it down. I saw the water being churned into a white froth by 20-mm cannon shells as the plane quickly went under. The fighters could have let this plane go; there was no way its crew could have escaped the harbor. But I guess they were so angry at what we were doing to them that they couldn't help themselves. The Germans had only one objective: destroying bombers and their crews.

Later, I heard that some British and American crews who parachuted into the Hamburg area that day were treated mercilessly. Some were bayoneted; others were hanged at the railroad station. Countless stories came back of the unfortunate Allied fliers who were caught.

Our own 96th Bomb Group lost seven Fortresses of the twenty-one that flew the mission. Coming back to England and landing that day was the exact opposite of the Le Bourget mission, when everyone had been exhilarated from the intense combat. Just the day before, we had seen air combat as defending ourselves, fending off attacks by German fighter planes. Today, it was clear that we had helped destroy a great city and kill many, many civilians. The shock of realizing what we had done penetrated all of us.

I silently thought of excuses. "I'm not the one who dropped the bombs," I said to myself. "The bombardier did that." But I couldn't ignore the fact that I had helped fight our way to the target and back, so that excuse didn't work. Then I tried not to think of what happened after we dropped our bombs, but I couldn't help picturing children down below. I told myself that they were fanatical young Nazis like the ones in the newsreels, tens of thousands of them, eyes shining, arms raised in salute to Hitler. But still, I thought, they were children.

Upon our return from this mission, the brass transferred us to the 337th Squadron, which had taken the brunt of the 96th Bomb Group's losses that day. We were also told to move to a newly empty hut, formerly occupied by three crews from the 413th Squadron who had been shot down. Another crew from the 413th moved in with us.

The next morning our scheduled briefing and mission were scrubbed. Hanging around and resting, I noticed a subtle change of attitude in almost everybody in the group. We had seen a lot over the last few days. There was no more rambunctiousness. The arguing and boasting and loud talk were gone. Everybody was quiet, though many voiced negative thoughts. Guys began to confide to each other that they wouldn't make it.

★   ★   ★

Around this time the other waist gunner, Russell Hubner, and I were cleared for an overnight pass. We decided to take a bus to a village about a dozen miles away. We went into a little pub where we had warm beer, which I did not particularly like, and asked where we could get accommodations for the night. The guy in the pub told us to go down the street to a private house where a woman would be happy to put us up for only a few coins. So we followed his directions and met the lady. She showed us a room with a bed with a down mattress. It was softer than anything I'd slept on in my life. The only problem was that when Hubner and I got into it, it collapsed in the middle and we were practically on top of each other.

The first thing Hubner did was take out all of his English money and spread it out on the table. He kept looking at it, wiping it, even washing it. Puzzled, I asked him, "What the hell are you doing with that money?" and he said, "I'm learning it." I replied that there was nothing to learn. I didn't need to know the difference between pence and half-pence and shillings and the pound and all that other stuff; money didn't bother me then and it doesn't to this day. But he wanted to keep looking at it.

I said, "Let's go to the pub and find something to eat. Maybe we'll meet some girls." We walked down a charming little lane toward the village, looked over, and saw two pretty English ladies sitting on a fence. They waved to us. We walked over and started talking, and they kidded us, asking where we were from. They had grown up in this little village. One had a boyfriend who was in the British Army in Africa. That became common. You'd meet a girl and her boyfriend would be in some other part of the world and here we were, in England and available. As the British put it, "The Yanks are overpaid, oversexed, and over here."

The Cold Blue Sky

English girls found sex very natural. No fuss, no bother, and almost always enjoyable. I remember my lady was blond, with blue eyes. Sex was easy with her, natural and wonderful. But afterward, Hubner and I went back to our rented room, and I had to spend the rest of a very uncomfortable night sleeping practically on top of Hubner. In the morning we woke up and headed back to the base.

Chapter Five

The interior of a B-17 was like a lightweight aluminum cigar tube. You could take a screwdriver and poke a hole through the thin skin almost anywhere. What gave the plane its extraordinary strength and its ability to absorb an amazing amount of punishment were the heavy-duty aluminum ribs, closely spaced and joined by thousands of rivets, that encircled and crisscrossed the inside of the cigar and supported the fuselage. Some of the aluminum was sharp, and we learned not to touch it in certain places.

Delicate steel cables that controlled the ailerons, elevators, flaps, and rudder ran the length of the fuselage at about eye level, held in place by hardwood blocks with holes drilled in them. You could see the cables moving as the pilot made his adjustments. If a bit of shrapnel cut some of the cables, the plane would careen out of control. Fortunately, this did not happen often—and never to our plane.

I had a considerable field of fire out of the opening on the left side, and the other waist gunner had an identical window on the right side. Each of us had a single-barreled .50-caliber machine gun mounted on a swivel. There was no flat floor, and we waist gunners had no place to sit. There was a platform maybe a foot and a half wide that we were supposed to stand on, but that was impossible because there were two of us fighting in the same space. We walked and fought on the curved floor, slipping and sliding in piles of spent brass shells casings that often reached above our ankles. It was not a user-friendly environment by any means.

Later models of the B-17 added some improvements: offset waist windows so that the gunners didn't get in each other's way; airfoils to deflect some of the wind from the openings; and eventually, enclosed waist gun emplacements in which the machine guns poked out through a clear plastic shield. But the B-17s Americans were flying in 1943 lacked these modern conveniences.

The Cold Blue Sky

Behind us was the tail section, through which the tail gunner crawled to reach his position and his twin .50-caliber machine guns. The tail gunner reclined in his narrow plexiglass compartment somewhat isolated from the rest of the crew. He was probably the most important gunner on the airplane. I'm sure that if you told a pilot he had to fly a mission with just one gunner, he would pick the tail gunner. If a tail gunner was killed or wounded and the enemy pilots saw it, that B-17 was almost a sitting duck. Whenever that happened, another crewman would quickly replace him, even if it meant unceremoniously pulling a wounded man —or a dead body—out of the way and jumping onto the gun.

Just in front of us—toward the front of the plane—were our oxygen cylinders and our radio jacks for the intercom. Then came the oxygen equipment and the hydraulic mounting for the ball turret gunner lodged in his little plexiglass blister on the underbelly of the plane.

In front of the ball turret was a door leading to the radio room. This wasn't really a room at all, just a niche on each side of the plane for the radio equipment. The radio man sat on the left side, facing the rear. Above him was an open hatch with a .50-caliber machine gun pointed up. The hatch afforded a somewhat limited field of fire, but many a radio man knocked down a German fighter as it overflew the formation.

Beyond the radio room was the bomb bay. Racks of bombs reached from floor to ceiling on both sides. To cross the bomb bay between the bomb racks, even a thin man had to walk sideways along an extremely narrow catwalk.

Forward of the bomb bay, just behind the cockpit, was the top turret gunner, whose bubble stuck up instead of down. Both the top and bottom turret gunners wielded powerful twin .50's. Both turrets were hydraulically controlled and could swivel 360 degrees. The turret gunners could shoot at an approaching fighter and then follow it, shooting continually, throughout the arc of its attack.

The top turret gunner was usually the plane's engineer and a technical sergeant, which made him the ranking noncom among the crew's six sergeants, all of whom were gunners. The other four members of a B-17's ten-man crew were officers: the pilot, the co-pilot, the bombardier, and the navigator.

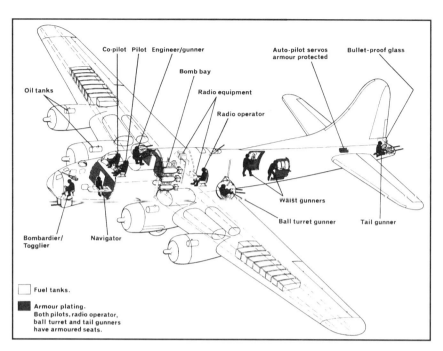

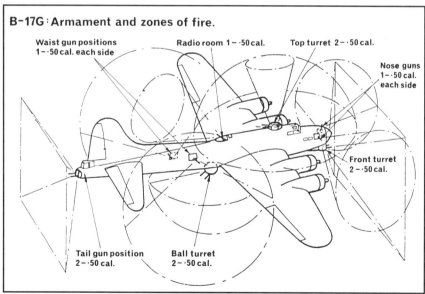

B-17G: Armament and zones of fire.

The B-17G shown in these diagrams has some features that were not found in the *Black Hawk* (an earlier model B-17F)—principally enclosed waist windows and a chin turret with twin guns. (Diagrams courtesy of Roger A. Freeman, from his book *Combat Profile: B-17G Flying Fortress in World War Two*, London: Ian Allan Ltd., 1990).

The Cold Blue Sky

In front of the bomb bay, you stepped up to the cockpit or down to the nose. Down a few short steps, the bombardier and navigator had the grandest view of all through the panels of their plexiglass compartment. The navigator sat at a small table with charts and instruments. Just a couple of steps away from him was a door for bailing out—that is, if the centrifugal force would allow you to get to it. Once a B-17 began spinning, it was virtually impossible to get out. And even if you made your way out this door, you had to be sure you plunged straight down to avoid being minced by the propellers. You also had to hope you would not get hit by the tail section, which happened many times.

The navigator had a .50-caliber machine gun on the left side of the nose. (Some crews had the armorers add a second .50 on the right side, and later models of the B-17 had both guns as a standard feature.) Below him, in the very front of the nose, sat the bombardier with his auxiliary controls and bombsight. He also had a .50-caliber machine gun. The bombardier used the top-secret Norden bombsight, the most accurate of its time. They told us it would shorten the war. The rest of us were acutely aware that the only reason we were there was to fight our way to the target so that the bombardier could drop the bombs. Then, of course, we had to fight our way back home again.

In short, the B-17 was not just a bomber, it was a formidable gunship as well. During a heavy attack, we could have everyone in the plane except the pilot and co-pilot firing away. The B-17 had no blind spots, so there were virtually no angles of attack that were safe for an attacking fighter.

B-17's could take plenty of punishment, too. They weren't invulnerable, but they were damned tough. The story of Captain Flagg's plane *Wabbit Twacks*, related in the previous chapter, proved that. Here's another example: On one of our practice missions, we were flying formation over England. (We dared not stray over the Channel because of the danger of being attacked by German fighters. Sometimes they even attacked our planes right over our base.) During this practice flight two light Mosquito bombers, twin-engine planes made in Canada out of plywood, dived through our formation. One hit one of our bombers and disintegrated like a wooden matchbox, leaving the B-17 completely unhurt.

Tactics also played an important role in combat missions. When the U.S. Eighth Air Force started its daylight raids on German-held Europe earlier in 1943, the bombers flew in a fairly flat formation. But when it became clear that this was contributing to very high losses, Colonel Curtis LeMay devised a formation of lead, high, and low squadrons in which our bombers were stacked and staggered into in a rough box shape. This famous "box formation" allowed the bombers to cover each other and, perhaps most important, to bring an intense, withering crossfire on attacking aircraft. Without the box formation, I am sure that our losses would have been even more severe than they were.

★   ★   ★

Almost before I realized it, I was a seasoned gunner, and our crew soon counted among the veterans simply by surviving. As for the long run, I tried not to think about my chances. But deep down, I was convinced that the odds would get me. No one was more surprised than I that we somehow lived through it all.

There's no doubt that our crew had far more than its share of luck. But something else played a part in our survival: We were good. Our crew worked like a well-oiled machine or a championship sports team, and that was why we did well in combat.

Our pilot, First Lieutenant James W. Tolbert, was born to fly. He was a lanky Oklahoman in his early thirties, which made him easily one of the oldest pilots in the group. When we became squadron leaders of the 337th, he was promoted to captain. He was superb at the controls of the plane. He could lead, or he could hang on to the element in front of him. He could fly a formation as tight as the Blue Angels'. In combat, if I asked him to drop down ten or fifteen feet to give me a better field of vision or line of fire, he would do it almost as soon as I spoke. I sincerely believe he was one of the main reasons our crew survived and finished its tour of duty. His skill, alertness, and cool head pulled us through many a tight situation.

Tolbert liked to drink, and they had a pretty good stock of liquor and beer down at the officers' club. There were many times when he seemed too drunk to fly—but he always could. We had a quick sobering-up system: You went down to the plane, put on a mask, and turned on the oxygen. The pure oxygen increased your metabolic rate and quickly burned off the alcohol in your blood.

The Cold Blue Sky

So no matter how drunk he was, by the time Tolbert had been in the airplane for a while and the motors were ready to be switched on, he was cold sober. Anyway, I'd rather fly with Tolbert drunk than with most other pilots sober.

Second Lieutenant Norman Macleod, our co-pilot, was in his mid-twenties. He joined our crew at Salinas, Kansas only days prior to our overseas flight, having just been discharged from the hospital. Macleod and an engineer had flown with a B-24 crew several months before, and the plane had crashed on takeoff. Macleod and the engineer were the only survivors, but Norman had been very badly burned around the neck and ears. I noticed that when Norman was worried about something, his ears were so transparent from the burn that they would turn red. Every time I saw Norman's ears turn red when we were flying a mission, I got scared, because I knew he was worried.

Norman was quiet and soft-spoken, kind and considerate. He was a very good co-pilot, and he got along well with Tolbert. I'm sure if an emergency had ever arisen and Tolbert had been incapacitated, Norman would have taken over and performed with a great deal of skill and coolness.

Down in the front end, in that big transparent nose, was Second Lieutenant Charles Blumenfeld, our skilled navigator. Charles was around twenty-three, a redhead and the only other Jewish boy on the plane. His main job was to take us to the target and back home again. He always knew precisely where we were—or at least that's what he told us. He called out the checkpoints. He was also the crew's monitor and reminded us to put on our oxygen masks as we reached 10,000 feet.

By the way, the fact that Charles and I were Jewish was never mentioned during our entire time in England. More than fifty years later, Charles remarked to me that he hadn't known I was Jewish until many years after the war. I recall only two conversations touching on Jews or Judaism while I was in the service. One was in Snetterton Heath. Early one morning I was riding in the truck out to the flight line for a mission, and sitting next to me was a guy from another crew. He remarked to me, "You know, I have 'H' (for Hebrew) stamped on my dog tags, and if I have to bail out over Germany, I'm going to throw them away." I replied, "I'm going to keep mine. I don't want to get shot as a spy." I never saw that guy again. The other time was earlier, while I was training in Rapid City, South Dakota. Some guy referred to another soldier as a "kike," and I said that I was Jewish, too. The guy shrugged it off by saying, "Yeah, but you're a white Jew," and we let it drop. Other than those times, the subject just never came up.

Blumenfeld had another job: his own private war bond drive. He constantly took pictures of the crew and our bombs and sent them home. If his parents or their friends bought a certain amount of war bonds, he would paint their names on a bomb to be dropped over Germany, take pictures of it, and send them home. Charles raised a lot of money that way. I can still see him chalking the names of war bond buyers on the bombs. It was impressive. I don't know how much money he raised for the war effort, but I'm sure it was a great deal. Thank God, Charles is still alive.

Lieutenant Lee MacDonald was our bombardier, but I never got to know him very well. We lost him on our second or third combat mission when he flew with another crew and was shot down. For years we thought he had been killed, but it turned out that he survived more than two years in a German prisoner-of-war camp and was liberated at the end of the war. He was replaced by Lieutenant Edward "Nocky" Johnson, a Brooklyn boy.

Our top turret gunner was supposed to be Sergeant Wilson Bills from Missoula, Montana. Bills was married and his wife was soon to give birth. He was one prince of a guy, but I knew him for only a short time because he was killed in action over Hamburg on his second mission. That was when our crew was being split up for our baptisms of fire. I flew that day in another plane in the same squadron, and I saw a load of bombs from another of our aircraft destroy his plane in flight. (By some trick of memory, I cannot recall the first name of his replacement, a man who I think was named Johnson, who flew with us on a dozen missions or more, and who is clearly shown in an old photograph of our crew.)

In the radio room was our skilled radio operator and gunner, Sergeant James Spell. He was from New Orleans and told funny stories in a wonderful Creole accent. Jimmy Spell loved the ladies, loved to drink, and was a warm, likable guy. We enjoyed him. He needled me mercilessly because I was the kid of the crew. I miss him.

Our ball turret or "belly" gunner, Ray "Dutch" Eisenhower, was from Pennsylvania and of "Pennsylvania Dutch"—in other

The Cold Blue Sky

words, German—descent. Small and thin, he fit wonderfully into the cramped ball turret. The fact that he could stand it was a tribute to his stoicism and self-control. Being in the ball turret was one of the most claustrophobic experiences imaginable. There he was, confined in that damned thing for three to ten hours, dependent on his oxygen mask and electrically-heated clothing. If something happened to the plane, he had to crank that ball turret around by hand, pop himself out into the plane's interior, and grab a parachute. The ball turret gunner couldn't keep a parachute on; there was simply no room.

Dutch and I were very good friends, even though he aggravated me. He was one of the neatest human beings I've ever known and so practical that it drove me nuts. But he was sweet and considerate, and I really liked him in spite of our different temperaments. I always worried about Dutch down there in that ball turret, and I made up my mind that if we got in trouble, I wouldn't leave the plane until I got Dutch out. Who knows if I would have actually done it?

Beside me in the waist was Russell A. Hubner, who joined our crew just before we left Salinas because the other waist gunner—whom I don't remember—left the crew there. Hubner and I spent some time together on leave. He was a very strange guy. When we were not scheduled to fly, he would go down to Operations to see whether he could fill a vacant place on a scheduled mission. Of course this greatly increased the odds that he'd be killed. He seemed to be the original war lover. After our fifth or sixth mission he went A.W.O.L., and three months went by before we heard of him again.

Then Hubner was brought into the base by the Military Police. His uniform was in tatters. He looked like he had a cataract in one eye, he was absolutely blind, and he was babbling. He was totally out of it. I never knew what happened. There were so many M.P.s all over England at that time that to walk around in a sloppy, dirty uniform and not be seen was physically impossible—unless somebody had been keeping him hidden somewhere. He was sent back to the States in a straitjacket and confined to an Army mental hospital for treatment. To this day, I don't know what happened to him.

Hubner was replaced by Dominic Beneditto—the guy who, on his first mission with his original crew, had been accidentally shot in the groin as I mentioned earlier. After his medical treatment and after Hubner left, Dominic became my partner in the waist. He was a dark, husky Philadelphian. I loved flying with Dominic. He never complained and had a good sense of humor. After the war we lost touch, and I have never seen or heard anything about him since then.

Our tail gunner was Victor Hunt. Hunt was a wiry, skinny guy of about twenty-two, a hell of a tail gunner and a hell of a ladies' man. He was a feisty one. We'd get into an argument once in a while, but we have remained good friends all these years.

About thirty years after the war, I was sitting in a crowded movie theater in Los Angeles with my wife. Five rows ahead, I could see the back of a man in silhouette. Without seeing his face, I said to my wife, "That's Hunt." How I knew who he was, I don't know. I got out of my seat, walked down to his row, got down on my knees and whispered, "Hunt?" "Yeah?" the man answered. I told him to come on out. We went out to the lobby where he recognized me, then we did a dance around each other and slapped each other's backs. As he went back to his seat he said, "Don't say anything to my wife about anything." We were wonderfully friendly for five minutes and that was it. And that was the last I saw of Hunt—until one day ten years later.

I was riding the cable car with my seven-year-old daughter in San Francisco, where we lived. The cable car was very crowded and this guy said to my daughter, "Honey, I'll move over, and you can sit there." The man was bald, pale, and a little heavy. All of a sudden, right before my eyes, the years melted away and again I saw the face of Hunt. I said, "My God, Vic Hunt." And he got up, and we exchanged telephone numbers and addresses, while the fascinated passengers watched. We keep in touch to this day.

After a time, the plane in which we flew most often as Tolbert's crew began to get a professional look. Bombs and Nazi swastikas had been painted beneath the window to signify the missions we'd been on and the German fighters which we had been officially credited for shooting down. (One was mine.)

When it came time to pick a name for our plane, somehow I got to choose, or at least the guys liked the name that I came up with. I called it *Black Hawk*—not for the Chicago Black Hawks, the hockey team, although I was from Chicago, but for the Blackhawk Indian tribe. I had read about the Blackhawk Indians and admired them. The others added their own ideas to the insignia, giving it individuality.

In the final design, a great big black hawk was carrying an eight ball, which had twin .50s sticking out of it as if it were a ball turret. The number eight stood for the Eighth Air Force, but to me the emblem had another meaning as well: At times, the odds on bombing missions were so stacked against us that I felt we were behind the 8-ball. The name *Black Hawk* was painted down below. It was an impressive and dramatic insignia, as pictures of our plane show. The art work was done by a talented guy named Johnny White who worked for Walt Disney before the war.

★   ★   ★

Every time we went to a mission briefing, we were told that what we were doing was shortening the war effort. They said we were saving countless lives which otherwise would be lost in the coming invasion of the Continent.

The flight surgeons and doctors told us that we had the eyes of eagles and the reflexes of cats. They said our organs and the passages in our body were superior to everyone else's because they weren't likely to collapse, explode, plug up, or otherwise cease to function in the thin air of 30,000 feet. On top of this we were supposed to have the emotional stability to keep our heads, do our jobs, and not become screaming claustrophobics when confined in a combat aircraft.

In return, we received an extra fifty percent of our base pay for flying and another twenty-five percent on top of that for flying combat. We were also in an assignment of our own choosing—a thing to be prized. In most of the armed services, a man who could shoot like Annie Oakley and liked to do it was apt to end up wasted as a mess cook, while the one who was best at making bread was likely to find himself inhabiting a foxhole.

We were a good crew, we respected each other, and we kept our cool. Nobody got hysterical, even in the heaviest combat conditions. We kept each other informed about where the enemy fighters were coming from. In spite of the hellish experiences we went through together, flying with these men was one of the great experiences of my life.

Chapter Six

Our crew was given a three-day pass to London. We cleaned up, put on our best uniforms, and caught the train. I was really looking forward to seeing London, having read about the city since I was a kid.

British railroad trains were smaller than ours back home, and the compartments opened separately to the outside. After a three-hour ride, we arrived at enormous Charing Cross Station, with a high, vaulted ceiling of glass that probably had not been cleaned in fifty years. Out we walked into London, where we immediately saw bombed and destroyed buildings—rubble from the Blitz and subsequent bombing by the Luftwaffe. This gave us a very eerie feeling; we in the Eighth Air Force were doing the same thing.

Everyone went his separate way except Dutch and me. We walked together and found ourselves looking at a huge old building alone in a wide expanse flattened by bombs. It was Saint Paul's Cathedral, its dome shining as if defying man's evil. It was a grand sight, the only thing standing in all that rubble.

As we walked around, we saw people from all over the world. They were wearing uniforms of every description and speaking languages I had never heard before. We walked past the Houses of Parliament and Westminster Abbey. I heard Big Ben striking, just as I used to during the early part of the war when I listened to Edward R. Murrow's show "London Calling" with the sound of bombs falling in the background. This was quite an experience for a kid from Chicago.

We had a pretty good dinner at a black market restaurant, then went to see a Noël Coward play. During the play, air raid sirens went off, and I started looking around to see where people were going to go. To my surprise, no one got up. Nobody left. The show continued.

The Cold Blue Sky

Dutch and I were quite nervous and wanted to go to a shelter, but we felt that as soldiers in uniform, we couldn't be the only ones to walk out. So we stayed and listened to the anti-aircraft guns and bombs dropping. Every once in a while the whole building would shake from a nearby blast. All in all, it was quite an evening at the theater. I never experienced anything quite like that again. It was a great example of stubborn British courage.

After the performance, we walked out into the blackout and fog and tried to find the little hotel near Hyde Park where we'd been assigned a place to sleep. Housing in London was so limited that certain small hotels were reserved for overnight lodging for officers and non-coms. We finally found it and turned in. We got up the next morning, had a cup of tea because coffee was impossible to find except back at the base, and caught the train. We felt refreshed from the London weekend. It was raining when we got back to base, so there was a chance the next day's mission would be scrubbed.

★   ★   ★

At times my fear was manageable. It made me quiet, but I could still ask or answer a question. At other times it was almost paralyzing, and all I could do was to put one foot in front of the other. According to the statistics, it was only a matter of time before I, too, became a victim of the air war. I saw our planes shot from the skies and blown up in the air. I saw comrades in arms bail out as their B-17s dived sickeningly into the sea. I watched as burning Fortresses twisted toward the earth, hoping to see parachutes appear. Were we next?

Of all the ways to die in a B-17, the one I feared most was the long, terrifying ride down from high altitude, unable to get out of the plane, waiting for the crash into the water or the ground. I was acutely aware that, in the case of ditching into the sea, I did not know how to swim. I knew the water was extremely cold and that death by hypothermia occurred after something like twenty minutes of immersion in the North Sea. I worried about bailing out of the plane and having the parachute malfunction or catch on the airplane. If the chute worked, I worried about being machine-gunned by a German fighter as I dangled there. I had seen it happen.

Chapter Six

My fear wasn't confined to what bullets and shrapnel could do. I was also afraid of what the cold alone could do to a man. One day when we weren't scheduled to fly, I was strolling toward my hut when I saw a navigator I had known from another crew. As he walked by me, I couldn't believe the sight. His face was totally eaten away. Even though his face was bandaged, I could see that his nose, one eye, one ear, and part of his mouth were all gone. I was horrified. I found out that he was in the nose compartment of his plane when the plexiglass was blown away. The cold air rushed in and tore off his oxygen mask and his helmet. His face froze.

On one mission our bombardier, Lieutenant Lee MacDonald, flew as replacement bombardier with another crew. A new man, "Nocky" Johnson, replaced MacDonald for our flight. MacDonald was shot down that day, and Johnson became our permanent replacement. Johnson had just gotten out of the hospital. His plane had ditched in the North Sea, and he was the only survivor from a life raft which started out with seven men. Everyone else died of hypothermia. They were in the raft three to four hours before British Air Sea Rescue picked them up. I think one of the reasons that Johnson survived was that he was quite a large man with a great deal of insulating fat.

We had a visit from an officer who was missing an arm and a leg. He had been repatriated by the Red Cross from a German prisoner-of-war hospital and camp as part of an exchange of badly-wounded prisoners. He told me a story about the sole survivor of an American bomber crew. After bailing out over Germany, the survivor was marched to the local jailhouse. Along the way he saw a batch of bloody coats and Mae West life jackets and recognized some of the names stenciled on the Mae Wests as members of his crew. He asked his captors what had happened to his crew, and he was told that they had been captured by civilians and stabbed to death with pitchforks. After hearing this story, I added another frightening way of dying to my personal list.

Then there was the takeoff for our mission to Kassell. It was still dark, and I was leaning up against the waist window, holding on as we thundered down the runway with an entire procession of bombers. Suddenly the whole sky ahead of us lit up and a tremendous boom shook the airplane. Later we found out that the plane just ahead of us couldn't take off. It crashed into a crossroads, killing every man on board and tossing one of the bodies into the kitchen window of a little village house, narrowly missing a woman who was making tea in the kitchen. I'm sure this was a hell of an experience for this lady. But for us, it was yet another way to die.

You could also be wounded or die by accident. There were incidents where a gun's safety was off and something—a piece of equipment, a radio wire—hit the trigger. You could easily shoot another plane in your squadron or even one of your own crewmen. It happened to others, and I had a near miss myself. On one early mission I accidentally fired a burst directly at the B-17 in front of us. I was sick with fear that I had killed some of our own men. However, the airplane flew on as if nothing had happened. Of course this did not prove that no one inside was wounded or dying. I worried about it all through the flight; even the distraction of combat didn't erase it from my mind. When we got back to base, I raced over to the other plane and asked if everyone was O.K. They said yes, they were fine. Then I examined the outside of the aircraft and found no bullet holes. Somehow I had missed—thank God. But I wondered how in the world I had, because it was a direct shot.

On another mission a B-17 flying on our left—my side—started to drop behind as we were leaving the target area. Two of its engines were smoking, and to lighten the load the crew started to throw out everything they could from the waist openings—extra ammo and even guns—so the plane could at least get out over the Channel where they could ditch and possibly be picked up by Air Sea Rescue. I wanted to do something for them, but I could only watch helplessly as they dropped behind.

★   ★   ★

Officers and non-coms in the B-17 crews were housed separately. In the non-com areas there were two or three crews—between twelve and eighteen men, all sergeants—in each hut. Our own hut had eighteen beds. These Nissen huts were made of corrugated iron in the form of a half-dome with a wooden wall and door at the front. The floor was concrete.

The hut we lived in squatted in the mud and looked like half of an old jelly roll turned gray with age. When you opened the door you saw unmade beds and crudely-fashioned shelves illuminated by a single bare light bulb hanging from a wire in the center. The shelves had odds and ends on them: family photos, pieces of shrapnel salvaged from planes, torn-up oxygen masks. The tiny coke stove in the center glowed, leaking smoke and not giving off much heat. The smell would have been atrocious, but we couldn't smell anything. We must have been desensitized from the constant stench.

At night the air inside the hut got quite smoky when the stove was going and chilly when it wasn't, even in summer. In the fall the huts became very cold. As the nights grew longer, the wet and chill of our metal walls and concrete floor became almost unbearable. We were issued a small ration of coke, enough to burn for only an hour or two. Everybody—*everybody!*—hunted for fuel. Outside the headquarters of our commander, Colonel Old, I broke into the coke bin and filled two buckets. The colonel would probably have shot me if he had caught me, but my buddies congratulated me for my daring deed.

We slept on a kind of a straw mattress covered with what the English called "ticking," a very heavy canvas-like material. We had no sheets or pillowcases. We had thick, itchy Army-issue woolen blankets. I don't recall anybody ever having a change of bedding the whole time we were there.

Then there was the ordeal of cleaning our uniforms. On top of the stove, we heated a bucket of 100-octane gasoline to the bubbling point. Everybody took turns boiling his uniform and then hanging it outside for the gasoline odor to dissipate. True, we were taking a big chance on the gasoline catching fire or blowing up, and a lot of the time the fumes inside were enough to drive us out. But it kept our uniforms clean of lice and crabs, which thrived in the damp English weather.

To take a bath or a shower, we had to hike about two miles to a bathhouse. It was punishing to do this in the wintertime, and as the weather got colder our hikes to the bathhouse dwindled to about once every two weeks. Inside, there was room for maybe six guys to shower. Hot water was limited, and there was no way to mix hot and cold, so the water was either very cold or very hot. Generally, you would get a little trickle to wash your head and barely dampen your body. Then you would towel off and hurry back to your hut. It would have been better to leave a bucket of water in the sunshine to warm up a bit. But there wasn't much sunshine. So we were stuck with this damp, moldy bath house with its primitive plumbing facilities.

Oddly enough, looking back I don't recall ever getting a haircut all the time I was in England, yet I must have. It's strange, because if I didn't have my hair cut, my helmet and oxygen mask never would have fit. So I must have gotten haircuts—maybe from some of the guys on the base, although I don't remember doing so. I know I didn't get any from an English barber.

The food was gruesome at our base. Some of the bases had good chow, but ours wasn't one of them. I wish our colonel had paid more attention to food. All I could get down before a mission was a piece of bread and some coffee. English bread was good—nourishing, thick, and solid. They'd bring it in by the truckload. Sometimes when I came back from a mission, all I could eat was coffee, bread, and some canned fruit. Thank God for the Del Monte's pears and peaches because at least, with the sugar and the fruit, I got some kind of nourishment.

In the hut we had an intercom system, called a "Tannoy," which was connected to headquarters. If headquarters wanted us to hear an announcement or something on the radio, they could broadcast it into our huts. I recall a mission when one of the crews in our hut went missing in action. That night we were listening to Lord Haw-Haw's regular evening summary. Lord Haw-Haw was a British turncoat who had gone over to the Germans. Often he had very accurate information. He would broadcast "welcomes" to new groups that had just arrived, names of airplanes shot down in flight, and all kinds of personal announcements.

That evening, we all jumped when he said, "You men in the 96th Bomb Group and in the 337th squadron, I'm sure that you're missing some of your friends tonight. Well, I've got news for you. Five of their bodies washed up and have been buried with German military courtesy, and five are prisoners of war." He proceeded to list the names. It seemed that there were no secrets; he knew exactly what we were doing. It was quite a shock, and it scared us.

Losses in crews and aircraft were mounting. Several crews living in our huts were killed or missing in action. At one point three crews from our hut had already come and gone and there were only five of us—all from the same crew—in our hut. Hubner was still A.W.O.L. Dominic had started flying with us, but he stayed in his old hut with people he knew better.

When a U.S. Eighth Air Force crew was listed as missing in action in 1943, the quartermaster came by after a day or two and picked up all their clothing and personal effects. During the interim before he came, looking at the photos and other things of your dead buddies was very demoralizing. The bunks could stay empty for up to a month. The R.A.F. had the right idea. They came by and cleared out the personal effects immediately. Furthermore, they had a "no-empty-seat" policy in the mess hall and everywhere else.

However distraught the deaths made us feel, if one of us had a worn-out leather jacket or other equipment, we were not too sentimental to avoid helping ourselves to better equipment. We knew our buddies would have wanted it that way; they had done so themselves in many cases.

We stopped making friends. For my own protection, I had decided not to memorize faces, not to look at anyone directly, and to keep my contact to brief hellos. I guess this attitude was part of being a veteran. That's how we had been greeted when we were new. They say it was the same among the ground troops.

I don't remember the faces of the new crews; they all became a blur. It seemed safer not to know about their girlfriends and their parents, or to hear about their dreams of marriage, jobs they wanted, or the good food they would eat—the milkshakes and the hot dogs and the steaks and the corn on the cob that they missed. We just didn't want to hear it any more. It would be too painful when they were shot down.

To get over the melancholy, when I had a little free time I would get on my bicycle and ride the beautiful country lanes that surrounded the air base in East Anglia. I'd stop and look at the magnificent old thirteenth- and fourteenth-century churches and at the gravestones out front which went back to dates like 1432 and 1562. On them were inscribed memorials to all those little tragedies which had happened so long ago, things like Mary-Beth died at seven, her beloved mother and father so forth and so on. The little church had its door open and its records available all the time. The sense of history of the parish was just fascinating to me. It was a fine place to be if one had to be anywhere in a war.

The Cold Blue Sky

On my bicycle rides I would stop at a canteen and share some tea with some of the personnel at a Royal Air Force base very close to where we were. We flew during the day, but the R.A.F. bombed at night. We envied their having the cover of darkness. We had no such protection. Most every evening, it felt like the whole of East Anglia was throbbing from the sound of R.A.F. Lancasters, Sterlings, and Halifaxes taking off for Germany. I wished them good luck, sweating with fear in their closed, cramped quarters. In the early morning some of their stragglers would land at our base in varying degrees of distress. We would see them at our early breakfast as we prepared to go where they had just been. East Anglia was one big aircraft carrier among the farms.

I wondered what it was like for some of those British flight crews, who were stationed near their boyhood homes, with families and friends right in the neighborhood—in stark contrast to most of the British and Commonwealth soldiers who were fighting in Burma, Africa, and God knows where. Who knows, maybe their being so close by and in such frequent contact made things even more stressful for their families.

We made friendships that lasted for the moment. We met girls; we took trips into Norwich to see a play; we enjoyed train rides to Cambridge. The farm work went on around us constantly. The cows sometimes brushed up against the corrugated huts at night, making a scratching noise that wouldn't let us sleep. The rats scurried about in the space between the outer and inner walls. It was all so different from my urban life in Chicago.

Later on, in October 1943, after the hut had been empty for a while, we relaxed our guard and became friendly with two new crews—Fabian's and Schroeder's crews. They had known each other for many months in training. They were a bunch of great guys. I really liked all of them, but now the only ones I can remember in Lieutenant Merle Schroeder's crew are Tex Shields, Johnny Hull, and Clarence Kelley. In Lieutenant George Fabian's crew I remember very well Tom Cole, Jay Epright, Truman Starr, and James Mabry. Of the other men I can't remember a face, not even an eyebrow. But of those I've named, faces, stances, and manners of speaking remain with me to this day.

Tex Shields was a very athletic, slender, clear-eyed Texan about my height, five feet nine inches or so. Johnny Hull was a dark-haired New Yorker and a wonderful talker who would regale us with stories. When Johnny and the rest of the enlisted men in Schroeder's crew first came into our hut to unpack, he pulled out a bottle of Johnny Walker Red Label Scotch and brought it to the other side of the hut. One door was used for exit and entry into the hut. The other was nailed shut, and there was a kind of a mantle on top of the door frame. Johnny Hull put that bottle of Scotch up there and said, "This is for New Year's Eve." (It was October.) Then he added, "I trust you guys not to touch it, and we'll drink a New Year's Eve celebration."

Clarence Kelley, a beautiful young man, was a blue-eyed blond from the small town of Bainbridge, Georgia. He was two or three years older than I and very quiet and soft-spoken. I remember many conversations with Clarence, ranging from racial problems in Georgia to just about everything else in the world. His father was a railroad conductor, and Kelley had worked as a bank clerk. Kelley was easily my favorite. I tried desperately to make good friends with him but somehow there was this little bit of distance that he managed to keep, not only with me but with everybody.

Joseph M. Tonko was a solid-looking, clear-eyed young man of twenty-four from Pennsylvania. Jay Epright used to sit on the top bunk. He was very pessimistic and always said that he wouldn't make it home alive. I used to tell him to shut up and not to be so negative. He would not listen to me when I told him that his chances were as good as ours. Then he'd sit back and say "Yeah? How good are they?" It was almost as if he knew his fate but had accepted it.

Starr was another live wire. I don't remember where Starr was from but I remember he was a dark-haired guy. Then there was Mabry, Shields' friend. Mabry got hold of a prewar British motorbike, and he would roar off on it many an evening and come home in the wee hours. Without fail, rain or shine, he was off on that motorbike. Whether he had one girlfriend, no girlfriends, or dozens of girlfriends, we didn't know. Nobody ever got anything out of him. He had one peculiar habit. Before every mission, he would prop up on his bed an envelope saying "My Last Will and Testament." But Mabry never showed any fear. In fact, none of us showed any fear, at least not outwardly—not even Epright with his constant lamenting that he wouldn't make it. Epright stated it as a matter of fact, not with any fear.

One time I rode with Mabry on his motorbike all the way to London. It was wild. I'd never experienced anything in my life like that, going down these narrow roads between hedgerows on a four-hour motorbike ride behind this wild man from Texas. He still wasn't used to driving on the left side of the road, so we roared down the middle. Thank God, because of wartime gasoline rationing, there was very little traffic. Otherwise, I think my Air Force life would have ended right then on that country road.

* * *

To get credit for a mission, we had to reach the main target or a secondary target, drop our bombs, and then come back. Once we flew to within an hour of Paris and had to abort the mission because of an engine malfunction. Although we flew back alone under extremely hazardous conditions and had a close brush with German fighters, we did not get credit for a mission. We were sometimes in the air as long as seven hours on combat missions that we had to abort. And the fewer missions on our record, the longer we would be away from home.

Once, as we took off in extremely bad weather at dawn, the mission was scrubbed. Along with three other planes in our flight, we tried to get back to the field, but the field was absolutely socked in. We tried to find another field close by, only to find that our radios weren't working. We flew for nine hours before we found the Burtonwood area, where there was a huge air force depot. On the way in we flew into a violent electrical storm and were tossed around like a leaf in the wind. Coming into the Burtonwood area under extremely heavy weather conditions, we almost crashed into the tall smokestacks surrounding the town. It took three passes before we finally made it. The tower was communicating with us not by radio but by flares. Green flares meant we were approaching correctly, red flares meant we were not.

A tricky part of this particular situation was that we were carrying new bombs with fuses that could not be taken out once they were inserted. With the earlier models of bombs, the Germans would sometimes salvage unexploded bombs by taking out the fuses. Now they couldn't do that without exploding the bombs—and themselves. We were supposed to dump the bombs over the Channel or anywhere over Germany but were not bring them back to England. But because we didn't know where we were, we dared not dump them. So we landed safely with this dangerous load of new bombs at Burtonwood Airport. It was almost as frightening as combat.

*   *   *

On July 30 we were sent on a mission to Kassell, an important industrial town in central Germany. Our target was the Fieseler Aircraft works, where they also made synthetic rubber. Kassell was well defended because of its importance to the German war effort.

We took off, heavily loaded with bombs, fuel, and ammunition, into a dark, rainy sky. Suddenly I heard a tremendous explosion, and the *Black Hawk* rocked from the turbulence as we swept over a ball of fire on the ground. The B-17 just ahead of us hadn't made it. After this harrowing beginning, we made formation with the rest of our group and our wing and headed toward Kassell. Near the target area we came under fairly heavy fighter attack. At times it seemed better to be engaged in action than to sit there idly and sweat and worry about it. At least it seemed that once I was occupied and fighting for my life, time passed faster, and I figured that what was going to happen had begun, and if we fought hard enough and were lucky, we would make it back to base.

We made a pretty good bomb run on Kassell and headed for home, with German fighters in pursuit. During one enemy pass, with six ME-109s barreling in on my side, I suddenly heard the crack of metal against metal and a great deal of rattling in the waist compartment—pieces of shrapnel flying around inside the plane. My oxygen went out, and I couldn't hear anything from the rest of the crew. I looked around and saw that all my wires had been cut, either by 20-mm cannon shells or flak. My oxygen cord was cut and the wires to my heated suit were cut. My electric communication wire was also cut, so I was out of contact with the crew except for Dominic Beneditto, the other waist gunner. I looked up and saw a huge hole just over my head where something had come into the airplane, probably shrapnel.

I noticed that I was bleeding slightly from my forehead. It didn't seem too bad, but I was starting to freeze to death. There was also an itchy sensation down below, somewhere around my stomach, but I didn't pay it much attention at that time because there was so much going on, so much distraction. Up in the air, unless the blood was visibly gushing or you could see an open wound, the cold, the excitement, and the thickness of our clothes prevented immediate discovery of a wound. I knew of one dead gunner whose body had been riddled with bullets, but no blood had shown until his outer garments were cut off.

I didn't think much had happened to me. My main concern was to keep from freezing to death for lack of wires to plug into my electric suit, but because we started to lower our altitude on the way back to the Dutch coast, I didn't think I had too much of a problem. At first I used the portable oxygen bottle to stay alive. After a while, I didn't need it any more. On our return flight, the fighter opposition soon turned away, and we didn't fly into flak. So we were in pretty good condition.

Then Dominic started looking me over. He looked at the floor over on his side. There was a hole right by his feet. He eye-balled the hole and then looked at the center of my chest. There was a hole in my parachute pack, a tiny bundle of silk. Generally I didn't wear my chute, but this time the action had been so heavy that I had put it on. I started digging my finger around in the hole, and black powder started falling out. I dug in some more and found the business end of a 20-mm shell that had somehow failed to explode.

Something had saved my life. That damned shell should have gone off on contact with the fuselage or at the very least with my chute pack. Yet all I had was a small stomach wound. The hole by Dominic's feet proved that the shell had come from the opposite side of the plane. For some reason I had turned around and taken that shot in the chest. If I'd been facing out my window, as I usually was, the shell would have hit me in the back and killed me.

I took that 20-mm shell back to our hut and put it on a shelf next to my bed. Every once in a while, I would look at it and marvel over my luck. One day, an armorer came to our hut looking for things guys were stashing away. He walked over to the shell and picked it up. Right away he said, "You know this damned thing is still live?" He took it away, and I never saw it again.

Following the Kassell mission I was hospitalized for a week or ten days for the stomach wound where a piece of flak or shrapnel had penetrated. Also, my feet had been frozen badly when my heated equipment had been shot out, and they hurt me worse than anything as they were thawing out. The pain was incredible, but it was still a relief to be in the hospital. At least I was safe for a while.

When the war was over and I got my discharge, I went to the Veterans Administration to get medication for my stomach and for frostbite pain. That first winter after the war was bitterly cold, and my frostbitten feet hurt a lot. I waited for three hours and then was interviewed by a doctor. "Another freeloader, eh?" he said. I was so furious that I pulled him over his desk, and I threw my discharge away after I left the building. (Later I went back and found it. A train had run over it, so I taped it together, and I still have it.) I never went back to the V.A. for anything. I just took aspirin. It is very hard to talk about this incident. I did not feel the government owed me anything; I always thought of myself as a solid American. I realized later that this doctor was not typical of the V.A. personnel.

⋆   ⋆   ⋆

Our crew got another brief leave in London. We took the train from Snetterton Heath to the big city, where we got off at Charing Cross Station and stood around awkwardly. I guess everyone had his own thoughts about what he wanted to do; anyway, we all split up and went our separate ways. "Dutch" Eisenhower and I went to the Hyde Park section where we got ourselves a room at an old club that had been converted into a billet for non-commissioned officers. We decided to walk down to the Soho theater district, where we bought tickets for another Noël Coward play. Then we walked around to look at the sights.

It was still light, and the streets were crowded. Servicemen from all over the world were there: South Africans, Poles, Free French, Norwegians, Canadians, and Americans—mostly air force and only a few infantry. I don't think they had begun the build-up for the Normandy invasion yet.

We were hungry and wanted to find a place to eat before the play. A couple of crewmen from another outfit directed us to a nearby black market place where you could get a piece of meat and some potatoes and stuff like that. We were pretty well fed for those times. The dinner had just a little piece of meat and cost each of us about six pounds, which I think was about $24.

Another leave didn't go so well. I had heard from home that my first cousin Bill was in England as a telegraph operator in one of the bomb groups. Bill was about my age, and we had gone to high school together. I had two days off and decided to visit him. I had to go by way of Cambridge. From Cambridge I was to take a train on to Ely. When I got to Cambridge, it was late in the afternoon, so I decided to find a place to stay that night and continue on early in the morning to the air base where my cousin was stationed.

I found a little hotel where a lot of sergeants were staying. The hotel must have dated back to the fifteenth century. I got my room key, then went out to eat and ended up with a little plate of ersatz fish and chips. I don't think there was much fresh fish coming in because fishing in the Channel was difficult and the Atlantic was heavily patrolled. Fishing boats didn't venture out too far.

I decided to take in a movie. In the lobby of the theater I met a very pretty girl. We decided to see the movie together and, as we were watching it, we began some very heavy petting. "My lucky night," I thought. "I'm going to have a lovely girlfriend to visit tonight." But as I came down to the lobby after the movie, her older sister walked up and snatched this beauty from me.

Disappointed, I went back to my hotel room and walked up the stairs. The hallway was so narrow that one person had to go sideways to walk. It was extremely dark. There was a bulb at the landing at one end, another bulb at the landing at the back, and no light in between. I was peering at the room numbers, trying to identify mine. All of a sudden, I sensed something behind me, and someone put his hand on my arm. A man's voice said, "Can I help you find your room?"

It didn't feel right. I looked around and shook his hand off my arm and said, "No, thank you, I can find it myself," and continued down the hall. I sensed something again and ducked. The stranger's fist caught me across my eye and tore my cheek open. I turned around to face a huge guy in U.S. Army uniform. I grabbed his head and we went down to the floor. We were wedged so tightly in the narrow hall that the walls held us like a vise.

Chapter Six

As my assailant struggled to his feet, he tried to get his hands around my neck. I kept forcing him down. He was groaning and grunting like an animal. There was a bathroom about three doors away; its door was open and the light was on. I hadn't noticed that before. Now this guy was trying to drag me towards the open bathroom. I had no idea what he wanted from me, but somehow I knew he would kill me if he got me there.

Still grappling with me, he tried to straighten up to get a stronger hold. He slowly inched his body toward the open doorway while I did everything I could to fight him. I couldn't get my arms around him because he was too big. I couldn't throw him off because he was too powerful. Meanwhile, I was trying to do as much damage to his head as I could because my hands were free. I had no room to punch; I could only tear and scratch at his face. I ripped one of his eyelids and tore the end of his mouth open. He was still grunting and groaning. Just then, at the end of the hallway, an elderly lady popped out of her door. I screamed at her, "For God's sake, get help!"

It seemed like a long time later, but finally she came running up the stairs with two M.P.s. They looked at us, and one said, "Hold it a minute." One stayed there while the other went back to the other stairway so that there was one at each end of the hallway. Then they told me to drop to the floor, and I did. The M.P.s charged in and started raining blows on his head with their clubs. They managed to drag him to the stairway at the end of the hallway, and there they stood, pouring blows into him. He was shaking his head, and white foam was coming from his mouth. I was so angry that I ran down the hallway and punched him full in the face. Finally, they subdued him enough to take him away.

The next day, the C.I.D.—the Army's criminal investigation department—took my deposition. Later I heard that they had my attacker locked in a mental ward nearby and that he was completely berserk. When I showed up the next day, my cousin looked at me and said, "My God, I'd heard from back home that you'd been wounded, but I didn't think you looked this bad!"

My face was swollen, my cheek was bleeding, my eye was cut open, and I looked like I had been through a meatgrinder. It was ironic that after going through some of the air war's heaviest combat, I almost got myself killed in a hotel hallway in Cambridge. To this day, I believe that he wanted to kill me, and I haven't the slightest idea why. It would really have been something for my parents to get a telegram saying, "Your son was killed in a hotel brawl in Cambridge, England."

Chapter Seven

We were past the middle of August, and the farmers all around our air base were beginning the harvest. Horse-drawn wagons crisscrossed the base, gathering the hay. Haystacks were everywhere. The big blueberry bush over by the edge of the field was in full bloom. Every time I'd go by, I'd stick my hands into the bush, pull out the gloriously sweet berries, and shove them into my mouth. These peaceful country scenes took me far away from the war for a few moments at a time.

We went on what should have been a comparatively easy run across the Channel to the French town of Abbéville. Since it was close to the coast, we had Spitfires as escorts, and they helped fight off an attack by an elite squad of German fighter planes, FW-190s. But the anti-aircraft fire was intense. Of the twenty-seven planes in our formation, twenty-one were damaged by flak, some of them severely. Somehow, we all got back—a tribute to the toughness of the B-17.

Then, one night, word came down that we were going on an unusual raid. They didn't tell us where, but they told us to pack toothbrushes. That was unusual, and I wondered what the hell it meant. The next morning, August 17, at briefing the red tape stretched all the way across the map to Regensburg, a city on the Danube in Bavaria (southern Germany). We were to be part of a two-pronged effort by the Eighth Air Force. We in the 96th Bomb Group were going to lead the Fourth Bomb Wing in the Regensburg raid. Our target was the Messerschmitt aircraft manufacturing plant. The other prong, the First Bomb Wing, was to take off about a half hour later to bomb the crucial ball bearing factories in Schweinfurt in central Germany.

Regensburg was 525 miles from our base in East Anglia. Up to then, our most distant target had been Kassell, only 200 miles from our base. Regensburg was so far away that we had to carry extra fuel in "Tokyo tanks" instead of half our bomb load. To confuse the German defenses, the brass had decided that after we bombed the target, our Fourth Bomb Wing would not return to England but would continue south, fly across the Alps and the Mediterranean Sea, and land in North Africa.

That day the Fourth Bomb Wing put 146 planes in the air, of which 126 were to continue to the target. The other twenty were spares which would replace bombers that dropped out early. We were all excited. Our group commander, Colonel Old, wanted to fly the lead plane, but he was bumped by the wing commander, Colonel Curtis LeMay. In turn, Colonel Old bumped the pilot of the deputy lead plane.

One of the reasons the planners wanted the First Bomb Wing to take off half an hour behind our Fourth Bomb Wing was to split the German fighter air force and lessen the blow for each of us. But fog and rain on the morning of the mission disrupted the timing. We were able to get off the ground and make formation in spite of the horrible weather. Both Colonel LeMay and Colonel Old had always insisted on practice—practice, and flying a tight formation. This was a day when practice paid off. But the First Bomb Wing had problems with the weather, and they ended up taking off two hours later. So the plan went out the window, and the Luftwaffe got a separate shot at each wing instead of having to divide its attention between them.

We crossed the Channel, the Dutch coast, and Holland, then headed for Regensburg. Over the Continent the weather was clear and beautiful. Below us the gorgeous German countryside, green and checkered, made a stunning panorama with glistening rivers and the Alps in the distance. It was hard to believe we were going to spread destruction on such a peaceful-looking landscape.

No sooner had that thought hit me than a huge swarm of enemy fighters came at us. I guess we were an hour or so out of Regensburg. It seemed as if we were under attack by the entire Luftwaffe. But our lead group was flying such a beautiful tight formation that the German fighters passed over us and started attacking the rear elements of our wing, which were spread out all over the sky. Incredibly, our group—the 96th—suffered not one casualty then or later that day. But for the rest of the Fourth Bomb

Wing, the ordeal had just begun. Over the next several hours, of its 126 B-17s, twenty-eight would be shot down.

Early in the battle, we shot down many of the fighters attacking us. But our rear elements had to fight through some of the worst combat of the war. When I looked back I could see parachutes, debris, German fighters, and American bombers scattered all over the sky, diving, smoking, burning, blowing up. It was a visual nightmare.

Then we made our bomb run, and the German attacks ceased. Soon we were flying over the beautiful Alps. We still had five hours to go. It started to get dark over the Mediterranean, and some of the planes were starting to run short of fuel, but we hit the African coast and landed in Algeria. We slept under the stars, lying in the sand beneath the B-17's wing and wondering about the Army Air Force crews that flew out of this hot, gritty countryside. England was a paradise compared to North Africa. But we didn't mind. We were all still alive.

We returned to England a week later, leaving behind another dozen B-17s that were too damaged to fly back. On our way we made a pass at the Luftwaffe field at Bordeaux-Mérignac. Three more of our planes went missing on this flight. Later, we were awarded a Presidential Citation for our part in the first American "shuttle bombing" mission. Back at our base, we learned that the First Bomb Wing had a disastrous time on its Schweinfurt mission: Thirty-six Flying Fortresses were shot down, twenty-seven of those that returned were damaged beyond repair, and ninety-five others were damaged.

One of the bomber crews in our group had bartered a pair of G.I. boots for a mascot, a tiny African donkey we called Lady Moe. They modified an oxygen mask to fit her and brought her back to England in their plane. The British authorities wanted to quarantine the animal because God knows what kind of diseases she could have brought into the air base, but the crew and the base personnel threatened an armed battle with the British authorities, and finally Lady Moe was allowed in.

She became everyone's pet and had total freedom of the base. She would come into the mess hall and eat cigarettes and food off the plates. I guess compared to North Africa, her life on the air base in England was extremely tranquil. When we left England, we gave her to a local farmer. Later, I heard she was killed by a train in 1962.

*   *   *

We had some leave coming, so our crew took off for London on a three-day pass. We were told to keep in touch with the base by means of a secret code. We would call our base operations officer and ask if some fictitious major was in. If they said he was in, we had to get back to the base because we were scheduled for a mission. If he wasn't, we could relax for another twenty-four hours.

When we got to London I split off by myself. I felt like being alone to wander around. I was happy not to have to be with anybody, just to walk along by myself. It was a typical London wartime evening, completely blacked out with the heavy fog swirling in. The coke that the British burned in their stoves and fireplaces created a disastrous smog. Because of the threat of air raids, every light was blacked out. Now and then I would get a glimpse of a light when someone pulled back a curtain to the entrance of a club, a restaurant, or a building lobby. There was a slice of wartime London in that flash of light.

After a long wait, I finally got a cab. I asked the driver if there was somewhere special he could take me for something good to eat. "Sure," he said, "Get in." The cab's headlights were masked, and tiny slits directed the beam down and straight ahead. Nobody could see the headlights because they illuminated only ten feet or so of the pavement directly in front of them. As a result, the cabbies had to go very slowly. But they had been driving cabs in London all their life, so they knew their landmarks and always know where they were in the pitch blackness.

We drove about three blocks, and he let me off. I paid him handsomely. At that time, as sergeants on combat pay and overseas pay, we were making about $230 per month—more than a British brigadier general. I had just been paid for the first time in months, so my pockets were bulging with pound notes.

I followed an older couple into the restaurant. He was a British naval officer with so much gold braid that I thought he must be an admiral—and here I was, an eighteen-year-old enlisted man walking into this restaurant in my khaki uniform with my sergeant's stripes and the blue patch of the Eighth Air Force. He wore rows and rows of medals; pinned onto my breast pocket, I had my gunner's badge, a Purple Heart for my stomach wound and frozen foot, and probably the Air Medal that everyone got after five missions.

The restaurant was elegant. The crystal chandelier sparkled, the white tablecloths gleamed, there were wine goblets on the table, and the china was exquisite. To top it off, the waiters were in tails. Most of the diners were older. There were women in evening gowns. I didn't see any other Americans or anyone besides myself with a rank below major.

The maître d'—although I wouldn't have known to call him that—seated me very courteously. I was a little bewildered. Back in Chicago, the only food I ever ate outside our house was a hot dog, a sandwich, or some smoked fish we'd pick up at Navy Pier on Lake Michigan. We couldn't afford to go out to restaurants other than local delis where we'd eat an occasional corned beef on rye. Restaurants with tablecloths were completely alien to me.

The maître d' seated me, handed me a menu, and left. The waiter came over, introduced himself, and left. I examined the menu. It was like a book—in French! The only thing I recognized was an omelette, so I went for that. The eggs we got in the service were powdered. Only once had we had fresh eggs. So I decided to settle for an omelette.

The sommelier—another word I didn't know—approached and asked if I would like some wine. And I said, "Yes, I'd like some red wine." The only wines I knew were Manischewitz and the other very sweet Kosher wines served on Jewish holidays.

He brought over a carafe of red wine, poured it into a gorgeous crystal glass, and waited. I took a sip and exclaimed, "My God!" I couldn't stand it so I spit it out into my napkin.

And he said, "What's wrong? What's wrong, Sergeant?"

I said, "The wine is spoiled. It's spoiled!"

"No," he said. "It's a beautiful dry wine."

He looked at me and seemed instinctively to understand my situation and how naive I was. He said, "Well, maybe we shouldn't give you this wine, I'll bring you something else." And he brought a tiny glass of sweet port wine. I told him that was much better. It was more to my taste. He was really nice to me. I can't think of many American waiters who would handle a situation like that with such grace and compassion.

Another waiter brought out an omelette made with vegetables. There was cereal mixed with it, but it was quite tasty. I paid my bill and walked out into the black fog to find a number of people waiting for a taxi. I was in no hurry, so I stepped aside and waited in the shadows. A taxi pulled up. Everyone screamed at him to stop but he continued on to where I was standing and said, "Get in, Yank." I told him to drop me off at a nice pub where something was happening. He took me around the corner and I gave him a pound, which was six bucks for this two-mnute ride. No wonder he passed by all those colonels and admirals and generals to give me a lift!

I walked into the very crowded pub—or club, I guess it was. People were singing around a piano. There were no Americans. They were all Royal Air Force. There were Canadians, New Zealanders, and men in the Free Polish Air Force. They were all singing and drinking and having a good time. When they saw my wings and Air Force badge they welcomed me with open arms. I ordered port.

We sang, and everybody told stories. They asked about my war experiences—how long I'd been flying and how was my training. Most of these guys flew in British Halifaxes and Lancasters. The R.A.F. bombed mostly at night—mainly because the planes were harder for German fighter pilots to see and, until radar was developed, harder for anti-aircraft guns to target from the ground. The R.A.F. made no claim to precision targeting; they did "general area bombing." Pathfinder bombers would fly in first and drop flares to light up the area. Then the stream of bombers would drop their bombs in the illuminated area.

I listened to the British pilots and crew talking about flying what I considered obsolete and inadequately-armed aircraft. They used .30-caliber machine guns whose accurate range was just a few hundred yards. Our much heavier .50-caliber machine guns were accurate to nearly 600 yards and had a maximum range of close to 1,000. In turn, they said we Yanks were crazy for flying in daylight bombing raids. Sometimes I had to agree with them on that score, but the daylight made our bombing more precise even though it markedly increased our losses.

A real camaraderie developed in the short time I spent with these R.A.F. pilots from all over the world. After the pub closed, I groggily set out into the blackout. I walked a little bit and managed to clear my head. Soon I found myself in Knightsbridge and made my way to my hotel. And there I lay down after a memorable night of drinking in old London town.

★   ★   ★

We were briefed to bomb Stuttgart on September 6. It was a heavily defended target featuring synthetic rubber and synthetic oil factories as well as a large railroad terminal. This was the day I discovered magic. I found I was able to transform into music the rattle of the airplane, the powerful throb of the engines, and the roar of the wind through the open waist windows. I was able to let the noise go into my ears and emerge in my mind as Rimsky-Korsakov, or Ravel's *Bolero*, or Lily Pons' sweet singing back in the park in summertime Chicago. I reveled in this new sensation for half an hour or so—until I was jolted back to reality by the intercom warning: "Fighters coming in at twelve o'clock high!"

For some reason unknown to us, our altitude that day was set at 17,000 feet. Normally, we bombed from between 23,000 and 33,000 feet both to stay out of the range of some of the smaller anti-aircraft guns and to make it harder for German fighters to dive on us from a higher altitude. The German planes weren't as efficient at high altitudes. At 17,000 feet, however, they could run rings around us.

It was a deadly day. The U.S. Eighth Air Force lost forty-five more bombers. We made our way to the target against fierce fighter opposition, and then we ran into exceptionally heavy and accurate flak. The Germans had lit thousands of zinc oxide smoke pots, completely obscuring Stuttgart from our sight. So after passing over the city twice, we turned west toward our secondary target, Strasbourg. We bombed the target and then tried to get out quickly. The smoke, flames, and heat were intense. Our eyes were watering from the smoke filtering under our goggles. Fortunately, nothing happened to our plane. I don't think the *Black Hawk* had even one hole, while fourteen of the aircraft around us—half of our group—suffered major damage.

We knew that the generals thought of us and our losses as statistics—sometimes acceptable statistics, sometimes not. Given the rate at which our bombers were going down, our chances of survival over half a dozen missions or more were not high. I tried not to think about the survival math. When I couldn't help thinking about it, I knew I'd never make it.

We made it safely back to base, landed, stowed our guns, and went to debriefing. I had my usual Spam sandwich at the Red Cross mobile wagon. Two women staffed the Red Cross wagon dispensing Spam sandwiches, hot coffee, and chocolate-flavored hot water with no milk: American servicemen weren't allowed to drink British milk because it wasn't checked for TB. Both of the ladies were in their thirties, and they were lovely. One, named Tatty, was the daughter of General Carl Spaatz, commander of the Eighth Air Force. They made a great effort to keep us happy and keep us going, to cheer us up and commiserate with us when we lost friends. They always knew by our looks what had happened that day.

It was still light after our debriefing. I put my flying gear in the locker and took a walk outside the base. After about an hour it was dark. I found it delightful walking there alone at night. I wandered past Eccles Pub where a lot of the guys congregated. I wasn't interested in the drinking or the evening camaraderie. After my walk I went back to the hut to wait and worry about what was going to happen next.

At the next morning's briefing, when we saw how short the flight was and where the target was, we all breathed a deep sigh of relief. It was a "milk run" to the French coast and back again, with the entire mission scheduled to take only three hours. It was close enough to England that we could have British Spitfires escort us to and even protect us over the target. About all we had to worry about was possible flak over the target.

This was a mysterious target. We were shown pictures of big rectangular concrete shapes among the trees. No one told us what these targets were, but we were ordered to drop our heaviest 2,000-pound bombs. We rendezvoused with the fast, graceful "Spits" just off the coast of France and flew to the target area, which turned out to have very few anti-aircraft guns. After this really easy run we came back to our base feeling like singing. Later, we found out that our target was the launching site for the pilotless V-1 "buzz bombs" that the Germans launched against London soon after D-Day.

The next mission was to Paris on September 9. We took off in formation and rendezvoused with the rest of the group. But as we crossed the French coast at an altitude of about 31,000 feet, our plane began to fall back. Our pilot, Lieutenant Tolbert, told us on the intercom that our superchargers weren't functioning, and at high altitude the engines weren't getting enough air. We continued to drop behind. When we were almost over Paris, we had no alternative but to turn around and come back home alone.

We hit the deck to make it more difficult for the German fighters to attack from above; at their diving speeds they would risk crashing into the ground. As we approached the French coast, Tolbert kept calling "Mayday! Mayday!" in hopes of finding some protection from patrolling British fighters. We were all scanning the skies for German planes. Then we flew right over a Luftwaffe base. I could see the planes roaring down the runway and lining up to take off. There must have been thirty of them. It wasn't hard to figure out that they were coming after us. We could smell the coast up ahead. We were really hightailing it, flat out at about 170 miles per hour.

Tolbert was still hollering "Mayday!" into the fighter channel and Spell was pounding out "S.O.S." on the radio. The German fighters were gaining altitude and were about to attack us. My fingers were ready at the trigger, my heart was pounding, and I thought to myself that this was going to be one hell of a fierce fight. All of a sudden, like corks popping up in water, more planes appeared, and we found ourselves surrounded by a squadron of Spitfires with the red-and-white Free Poland insignia. A pilot with a white silk scarf grinned at me and gave me the thumbs-up. I saluted him in return, overwhelmed with joy and relief.

Not much that I've seen in my life has looked as good as those Polish pilots in their British planes. Without a doubt, they saved our lives. They escorted us out of danger, across the Channel, and home. As for our mission, it went down as aborted because of mechanical problems. In other words, it didn't count.

* * *

Our flight surgeon, Captain Sam "Doc" Hartman, was a very compassionate person, kind through and through, and brave to boot. He flew as many missions with us as the brass would allow, including that rough mission to Le Bourget. His integrity and courage inspired the rest of us.

Around this time, Doc Hartman decided to send us to the flak farm, otherwise known as the rest home. During our tour of duty we were sent to rest homes several times. There were many of them around, and some were wonderful, especially the country estates which had been turned over to the Eighth Air Force medical personnel. Some were on farms and had wonderful food—milk, eggs, butter, chickens, and beef.

But this time we were sent to Blackpool, an old Victorian resort on the west coast of England. The miserable fall weather was bleak. The Irish Sea was cold and gray, and we could feel the wind even when we were inside our eighteenth-century hotel. The food was awful. Still, we didn't have to fly that week, and that was enough to keep us happy for a while.

★   ★   ★

We were pretty informal around the base. About the only person for whom we came to attention was our group commander, Colonel Archie Old, when he came into the briefing room. Other than that, we showed none of the military courtesy required between enlisted personnel and officers. For example, we never saluted the pilot, our crew commander. I addressed my pilot, Lieutenant (later Captain) Tolbert, as "Sir," not so much because he was an officer but because he was senior in age and boss of the crew. I didn't call the navigator or the co-pilot or the bombardier "Sir," although they were all officers. Like everyone else, I addressed them by their first names.

I remember an occasion when we were awakened at 0300 hours, went to briefing, and then were told that the mission was canceled because of weather conditions. We were tired; we had flown a mission the previous day. So we went back to our hut to catch up on our sleep. Around 1000 hours the door opened and somebody yelled, "Atten-shun!" We looked up out of the bed and saw a full colonel at the door with a major and two M.P.s. He was yelling, "Atten-shun." In our groggy state, not one of us moved.

Then the colonel said to the M.P.s, "I want these men lined up and placed under arrest." He was screaming at the top of his lungs. We found out that he was from the Inspector General's office. We had never had any kind of an inspection while we were in combat. It was something that just didn't happen. Our purpose was to fly, fight, and die. Who was this silly ass anyway? Didn't he know we were risking our lives every day?

Over came Lieutenant Colonel James L. Travis, our new group commander. He wanted to find out what was going on and got into an argument with this inspector-colonel. Finally they got hold of Colonel Old, who had been promoted to staff duty at the 45th Combat Bombardment Wing (which had taken the place of our old Fourth Bomb Wing in an organizational reshuffle) but whose new office was right on the base at Snetterton Heath.

Colonel Old took the inspector aside and explained the facts of life to him. First of all, the inspector should have come to Colonel Old and introduced himself. Colonel Old didn't welcome intrusions on his base. He also explained that because of the danger of being taken prisoner, to be on a flight crew a soldier had to be at least a buck sergeant. According to the rules of war, non-commissioned officers who were taken prisoner were not subject to P.O.W. labor camps. If a crew member was busted below sergeant in rank for whatever reason, he couldn't fly. Colonel Old continued that this was a combat base and, since there was a shortage of personnel to fly combat, the crewmen were in a win-win position. If we were going to be flying, they couldn't do much to us. If they busted us, we wouldn't be flying.

This amusing incident—all of which took place within our hearing—was, for us, high comic relief. Of course the service is full of self-important jerks. But after facing ME-109s, we were in no mood for boot-camp B.S. on the part of some creep colonel.

★   ★   ★

One of our most memorable missions was another flight to Paris on September 15. Our target was the Hispano-Suisa works, where intelligence reported the Germans were manufacturing ball bearings as well as tank and airplane engines. It was part of the Renault factory complex on the Seine just southwest of Paris. Our I.P. (initial point) was the Eiffel Tower. We were going to line up on the Arc de Triomphe and the Champs-Élysées, the great boulevard that I would walk many times in the future, make a right turn over the Eiffel Tower, and head for the target. To minimize deaths of French civilians, we were scheduled to bomb it at the noon hour when, according to our intelligence sources, most of the workers would be gone for lunch.

After briefing I was called aside and issued a big bulky camera in a protective case. It was called a K-10, and it took pictures with a depth of field from zero to infinity. All I had to do was aim it, press the trigger, and take pictures of what I thought might be interesting. Then I was to bring it back to the camera shop so the film could be developed for intelligence purposes. I was designated keeper of the camera—at least while I was not shooting at ME-109s.

Off we went to Paris again, fully expecting the heavy opposition we had encountered last time. It was a gloriously clear, sunny day. Just before we reached the city, we came under attack by about twenty German fighters. I was leaning against my gun, looking out when, all of a sudden, right in front of me appeared an ME-109. It must have reached the top of its climb and there it was, tucked in between our wingtip and our tail, stalled out and seeming to stand still. I swear that if my gun had been three feet longer, I could have touched the fighter with it. I could see the pilot looking at me through the canopy. I let loose a burst from my .50-caliber machine gun, and shells exploded around the cockpit. There seemed to be a fine mist in the air like gasoline from a nozzle and the German plane caught fire.

The pilot blew his canopy off and ejected. His suit was on fire. His parachute opened up, burned away in an orange-yellow blaze and he came out mouthing a scream. As he came out of that thing he seemed to turn and look at me again before silently falling. Then he plummeted to earth like a character called the Flame Man in a comic strip I used to read. I'll never forget the image of him freezing in front of me in slow motion. It was as if time stopped. It took me more than thirty years to forget that horrible moment. I can only hope the pilot was dead before he started to fall in flames —but I don't think he was.

We were approaching Paris and the Eiffel Tower. A group ahead of us had already made the turn toward the Hispano-Suisa works and had come under extremely heavy flak attack. The entire sky over Paris was covered with black puffs. We came into the same flak prior to reaching the I.P. The blasts were deafening, and the explosions were so heavy that the *Black Hawk* was like a dog being shaken by the neck. Holes began appearing all over the plane, including the wings.

Looking down, I saw three of our planes crash into apartments along the main boulevard of the Champs-Élysées. Then the Fortress on our left, *Pat Hand,* piloted by Lieutenant Ken Murphy, caught a direct flak burst and started to go down with flames streaming from its wings. I pulled out the camera and aimed it. The stricken bomber was a couple of thousand feet below us when I snapped a picture that, unbeknownst to me, became a classic of the air war. After I took the photo, we made the I.P. and carried out our bomb run. I didn't learn about the photo until a couple of years later, when the Eighth Air Force published a book called *Target Germany,* later republished by *Yank Magazine.* That photo was in that book. It's now in our unit history photo records. Even though my name isn't on it, I know I took the picture because I was the only one in position to do so at the time.

The next time I flew over Paris was maybe twenty years after the war. As we circled over the city in preparation for landing, I saw the Eiffel Tower and it all came back to me. To this day I can remember how the Eiffel Tower and the boulevards looked down below. A year after this mission, when I was in Florida at a rest and rehabilitation facility, I was having a beer with a gunnery sergeant who had been shot down and had made contact with the French Underground. He had been in a safe house that day in Paris sitting on a balcony having a glass of wine as we flew in. He was calmly watching what was happening up above. He said he was happy to be on the ground watching!

Our bombing of the Hispano-Suisa factory was one of the most successful bombing missions of the war. We totally destroyed the plant, but the loss of French life was minimal. Somehow, about two days later, our intelligence obtained pictures taken by the French Underground. The photos showed the damage done to the factory by our accurate precision bombing.

It was another tired, subdued bomb group that came back to base that day. We went to bed exhausted. But we flew again the next day, September 16. Our primary targets were in the Bordeaux area. It was an eleven-hour, 1,600-mile round trip. We flew at low level almost all the way. It was exciting to fly across Cornwall at treetop level and then zoom over the beaches where the Sunday crowds were out. It must have been an impressive sight from the ground. We could see the people waving to us as our Flying Fortresses roared right over them and headed out to sea. It was wonderful to be warm and not on oxygen. I could smell the ocean and see schools of fish beneath me.

The Bordeaux targets were obscured by thick overcast, so we turned back toward Brittany to hit the same submarine pens at La Pallice which had been the target on one of my first combat missions in July. After many hours of low flying, we went up to about 13,000 feet to make our successful bombing run over the submarine pens. We met hardly any opposition. Then we went back down on the deck and headed home. It was hard to keep a proper formation at such low altitude, and we were strung out all over the ocean. All of a sudden, we heard firing at twelve o'clock, rear, low. We were under attack by long-range JU-88s and quickly tried to tighten up. One plane in our group had two gunners, Donald Partridge and George Ferris, on their twenty-fifth and final missions. Each lost a leg. But all of our planes got home. We flew over London right among the barrage balloons. We didn't get back to our base until midnight.

On this mission a waist gunner temporarily assigned from a new crew flew his first mission with us—and slept most of the way. I kicked him awake over the target, and then he went to sleep again. This dumb jerk told me if this was combat, he would sleep his tour away. He had a lot to learn. He was one startled human when the JU-88s attacked. As angry at him as I was, I was not happy that he and his crew were shot down on their next mission.

That reminds me of another replacement waist gunner, one who flew with us after Hubner went A.W.O.L. and before Dominic joined us. This guy brought a couple of bricks along on a mission. While we were waiting to take off he used a heavy crayon to write on the bricks. He put down his own name and rank and little sayings to the Führer and very derogatory things about the Germans.

"What are you going to do with those?" I asked.

"Well," he said, "when we have a free moment over the target area I'm going to drop one of these bricks and maybe it'll hit something vital."

"Well," I asked, "did you ever think one might land intact and fall into the Gestapo headquarters? They'll have you on their shit list and if you get caught there you'll have that brick with your name on it just waiting for you." He decided he wasn't going to drop any more bricks!

On this mission, that same gunner had the tips of the forefingers on his right hand shot off just below the nail. The wounds were so clean that they hardly bled. I put a bandage over his hands and gave him a shot of morphine, but he seemed to be okay. He went into the hospital and came out again and was put back on combat duty. He had enough fingers and joints left so that he could still fire. He could still use his trigger finger. Strangely, on his very next mission he had the same hand shot away to just below the second knuckle and it disqualified him from flying as a gunner. It was the most extraordinary incident.

*   *   *

On one mission—it may have been to Emden, Germany, in late September—we flew unusually high, leaving England at 33,000 feet. To this day I don't know if it was fear, or something I ate, or the fact that I didn't eat, but the minute we got up to that altitude, the cramps in my feet and in my stomach and my ankles were so incredible that I had to lie down. Dominic, the other gunner, came over to ask me what was happening. I was in so much pain I could hardly talk. I called the pilot on the intercom and told him I was in such incredible pain that I was going to put on my chute and jump out. Later, I found out that I was suffering from some kind of reverse "bends." Divers get "the bends" when the increased underwater pressure changes the chemical composition of their blood. But I was up high, where there is less pressure and where expansion of dissolved gases in the blood can sometimes cause this phenomenon. As I learned, it happened to a few other guys.

The pain was so intense that I was out of my mind. I had to be restrained by Dominic and Jimmy Spell from jumping out of the plane. At that altitude I was useless as a gunner, and that made the plane vulnerable. Either the plane had to descend to a lower altitude immediately, or it had to turn around and come home. Descending meant flying alone and out of formation and risking being shot down. *Black Hawk* turned around and came home. Of course that meant that none of the crew got credit for a mission.

I was mortified and disgusted with myself, because I didn't know whether it was fear that had made me turn around, or whether there was actually something wrong with me. I have tried to evaluate my situation at that moment honestly, and all I know is that the pain was so intense that I was actually willing to jump out of the plane at that altitude just to get relief.

★   ★   ★

Before I began flying, I always had an insane fear of heights. If I got to the top of a building, I couldn't force myself to go to the parapet and look down without becoming extremely nervous. If I was at the edge of a cliff, I couldn't peer over the edge. I almost had to have somebody hold me. Yet in the airplane I could look out of the window, stick my head out, walk over to the bomb bay with the bomb bay doors open, and look down from 30,000 feet without being bothered. I don't know why. Maybe it was because the plane wasn't attached to the ground. But if it had been otherwise, I never could have flown. To this day I can't go up on a high building or come to the edge of a cliff without experiencing irrational fear. But I like flying. It's very strange.

During my time in B-17s I preferred low-level flying, though we didn't do it often. At high altitude we were in an alien world detached from the earth way below, with only the guns of the enemy trying to force us to the ground. I loved to fly close to the ground where the sensation of speed was thrilling. We did this only twice in training: once taking photos of Mount Rushmore, and the other time flying from Pierre, South Dakota to Kansas City. We flew right down on the Missouri River with the water almost lapping the bottom of the plane and the banks of the river flashing by below us.

Then in England we flew low over the beaches of Cornwall to avoid being picked up by German radar. I could feel the warmth and breathe the air and see life flashing beneath us, horses, cows, people, cars. Coming home late in the day from another mission, we flew low over London, threading our way among the barrage balloons. To discourage the Luftwaffe, these balloons were spread out all over the city and tethered by steel cables that would bring down a low-flying plane. In the gathering dusk Tolbert banked the *Black Hawk* again and again, weaving in and out to avoid the cables. I was hanging on to the lower ledge of my waist window, thrilled by the sensation and the sights as the cityscape flashed by below us.

A B-17 waist gunner in action. *(Peter M. Bowers Collection)*

Above: Jack Novey (r.) and fellow gunner trainees Tony Harkey (l.) and William Powell, Rapid City, S.D., winter 1942-43. *(Jack Novey)*

Below: Gunner trainees Jack Novey (l.) and Harry Brown on the train to Spokane, October 1942. A young girl snapped this shot from the platform and later sent it to Jack. *(Jack Novey)*

Above: The *Black Hawk's* distinctive nose art was painted by Johnny White, a former Disney artist. *(96th Bomb Group Museum/Geoff Ward)*

Below: Crew of the *Black Hawk,* from left: Lt. Edward "Nocky" Johnson, Jack Novey (squatting), James Spell, Dominic Beneditto, Lt. Charles Blumenfeld, Capt. James Tolbert (sitting), Lt. Norman Macleod, Ray "Dutch" Eisenhower (squatting), Vic Hunt, and the top turret gunner, who was named Johnson. *(96th Bomb Group Museum/Geoff Ward)*

Above: Lt. Charles Blumenfeld (l.) and Capt. James Tolbert point to messages paid for by purchasers of war bonds. *(Charles Blumenfeld)*

Below: Ground crew of the *Black Hawk.* Crew chief Johnny Euhas (l.) later became a gunner. *(96th Bomb Group Museum/Geoff Ward)*

Above: Wartime aerial view of Snetterton Heath Airfield, base of the 96th Bomb Group. Runways are at the far left. Three B-17s are parked in the 337th Bomb Squadron's dispersal area near the center of the photo. *(96th Bomb Group Museum/Geoff Ward)*

Below: Nissen huts (enlisted men's quarters) at Snetterton Heath after a rare snowfall. *(96th Bomb Group Museum/Geoff Ward)*

Above: This B-17, *Kipling's Error*, was typical of the 96th Bomb Group's planes. Jack Novey flew some of his early missions in this Fortress. *(96th Bomb Group Museum/Geoff Ward)*

Below: A ground crew tends an Eighth Air Force B-17. *(96th Bomb Group Museum/Geoff Ward)*

Fortresses of the 96th Bomb Group cross the Alps on the Regensburg shuttle mission, Aug. 17, 1943. (*U.S. Air Force Academy Library*)

Above: A B-17 suffers a direct hit by an anti-aircraft shell. *(U.S. Air Force)*

Below: Lady Moe, the 96th Bomb Group's mascot brought back from North Africa on the shuttle mission, joins the enlisted men's chow line. *(96th Bomb Group Museum/Geoff Ward)*

Above: A squadron of the 96th Bomb Group drops bombs simultaneously by keying on the lead plane's release. *(96th Bomb Group Museum/Geoff Ward)*

Below: A bomber crew is debriefed after a mission. *(U.S. Air Force)*

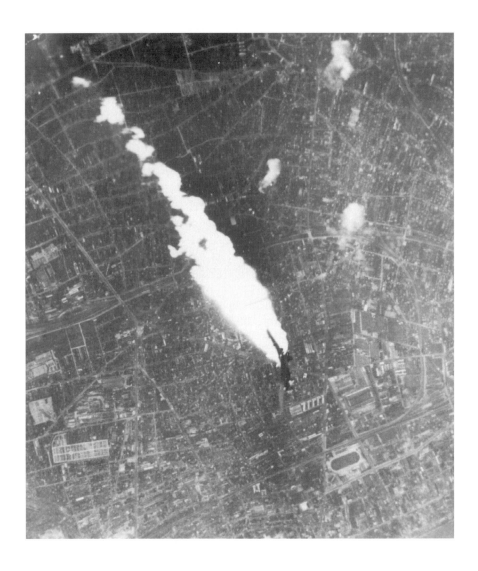

Jack Novey snapped this photo of *Pat Hand,* a B-17 from his own 337th Bomb Squadron, going down in flames over Paris. *(96th Bomb Group Museum/Geoff Ward)*

A B-17 of the 96th Bomb Group over England. This Fortress has a chin turret under the nose. (*U.S. Air Force Academy Library*)

Above: The 96th Bomb Group sets out for Bremen, Oct. 8, 1943. *(96th Bomb Group Museum/Geoff Ward)*

Below: Bombs Away! A Fortress of the 96th unloads over Bremen. *(96th Bomb Group Museum/Geoff Ward)*

German smokepots fail to hide the Bremen railyards from American B-17s, Oct. 8, 1943. *(U.S. Air Force)*

Above: Schweinfurt burning, Oct. 14, 1943. The Eighth Air Force lost sixty B-17s on this strike against German ball-bearing plants. *(U.S. Air Force)*

Below: American P-51 "Mustang" fighters with drop tanks were all too rare a sight for bomber crews in 1943. *(U.S. Air Force)*

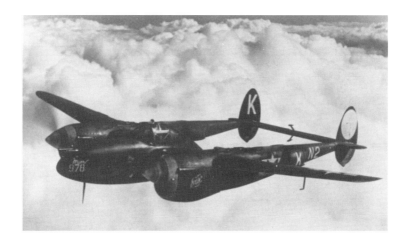

Three American planes of World War Two. *Top:* B-24 "Liberator" heavy bomber. *Middle:* P-38 "Lightning" fighter. *Bottom:* P-47 "Thunderbolt" fighter. *(U.S. Air Force Academy Library)*

Two of the best German fighters. *Above:* Messerschmitt Bf-109, popularly known as the Me-109. *Below:* Focke-Wulf 190. *(U.S. Air Force)*

A Fortress goes down in flames. *(U.S. Air Force Academy Library)*

Above: Kipling's Error, a B-17 of the 96th Bomb Group, with flak bursts in the background. *(96th Bomb Group Museum/Geoff Ward)*

Below: A B-17 drops a load of incendiary "stick" bombs. *(U.S. Air Force Academy Library)*

High and cold over Norway. A B-17 of the 96th Bomb Group on the Rjukan mission, Nov. 16, 1943. (*96th Bomb Group Museum/Geoff Ward*)

Above: Four men died when the *Dottie J II,* piloted by Lt. George Fabian, crashed at Snetterton Heath on Dec. 13, 1943. *(96th Bomb Group Museum/Geoff Ward)*

Below: The six enlisted men of Lt. Merle Schroeder's plane (l. to r.): Anthony Carpentieri, Arthur Demieux, William E. "Tex" Shields, Jr., Richard Rucker, John B. Hull, Jr., Clarence Kelley. *(96th Bomb Group Museum/Geoff Ward)*

Above: Out of control, a stricken B-17 plunges earthward. *(U.S. Air Force)*
Below: Sgt. Jack Novey in Florida, spring 1944. *(Jack Novey)*

Jack Novey (l.) and Norman Macleod at the 96th Bomb Group Museum, Snetterton Heath, 1992. (*Eastern Daily Press*)

Tex Shields at the grave of James W. Mabry, his friend and fellow Texan, in Cambridge American Cemetery and Memorial at Madingley, Cambridge, England, 1992. (*Jack Novey*)

Above: The site of Snetterton Heath Airfield has returned to farmland. *(Jack Novey)*

Below: Jack Novey beside a touring B-17 in 1995. Back in 1943 his waist window was wide open, unlike the one in this later model Fortress. *(Jack Novey)*

Statue of a gunner stands along the Wall of the Missing in Cambridge American Cemetery at Madingley, Cambridge, England. *(Jack Novey)*

Chapter Eight

We fought together as a crew, but privately and socially we went our own ways. We went on pass separately, except one night when three crews—ours, Fabian's and Schroeder's —went into Norwich together to see a musical. We sat in one great big bunch, thirty of us, and watched the little amateur show. All the cast was in costume, the scene was colorful, and the plush little theater was bright and beautiful. After a very enjoyable evening, we all jumped a truck going back to the base, feeling pretty good.

We searched constantly for some kind of entertainment. There was one local jazz club, but I rarely went there. The base had a new N.C.O.s' club called Duffy's Tavern. We'd go there sometimes in the evening to sit and be with each other. A guy would play the piano, and there'd be little songfests.

Our group, the 96th, had a little band; they rehearsed and occasionally threw a dance. The band was quite good, but the dances were infrequent. All the time I was there, nearly a year, there were only two. They would empty out one of the hangars and bring in busloads of women from surrounding communities like Norwich, or from a British Army camp for female military personnel (the equivalent of our W.A.V.E.S.), and there would be dancing and lovemaking.

Everybody was lonely, and lovemaking came easy. It was part of life then. The ladies came in all sizes and shapes. The men at the base, flight crews, ground crews, officers, and enlisted men were all competing with each other. It was much-needed fun for most of the guys. As for me, I would try to mingle, but I just couldn't blend in. There were too many missing faces, so I would go back to the hut or visit my local girlfriend.

Most of the guys I talked to never discussed the future. They talked about what was happening back home, and sometimes they mentioned girlfriends. They didn't talk about politics, they didn't talk about the danger of the air war, they didn't talk much about anything. They didn't talk about food. It was a far cry from war movies, where guys in the trenches are slogging through the mud talking about the good eats they're going to have when they get back home. They never talked about that. They kept most of their thoughts private. Sometimes there was a little bit of barracks humor about sex, but that was about it. Maybe it was because, deep down, we believed we had no future.

Some of the guys found the loves of their lives around the base. One of them was Johnny Euhas, our ground crew chief. He had a very secret girlfriend whom he never allowed anybody to meet. She would come and meet him sometimes by the gate when none of us were around. He was obviously happy and very close to her, and she was close to him. It was a very strange romantic interlude in his life.

Johnny was a Pennsylvanian of Polish-Russian descent. He bemoaned the fact that, if we finished our tour of duty, we'd get to go home and he'd have to stay for the rest of the war. At that time, in 1943, the war might go on for ten more years for all we knew, and Euhas thought he might be there for years. So I always used to kid Johnny, "You're a trained engineer crew chief. Go to The Wash and get some gunnery training, and I'm sure we'll find a crew position for you as a top turret gunner." (The Wash had an Eighth Air Force gunnery school.) One day he said to me, "Jack, I've applied for gunnery training, I'm going to The Wash." "Dear God," I thought. And as it turned out, later on he did join our crew as a gunner.

There were not too many married guys around. Blumenfeld had been married in Rapid City, South Dakota to his wife, Ethel, and we all went to the wedding just prior to our leaving for overseas. Bills, recently killed in action, had been married just before he had left for overseas and his wife was pregnant. Later on she had a girl.

I don't know if James Spell was married or not. He made me think he might have been, but he had numerous casual affairs. One night he came in from town at about two o'clock in the morning, sobbing out loud. I turned on the light and said, "Jimmy, what's the matter?"

94

He answered, "I'm sick."

I said, "What's the matter?"

"I have the clap," he said.

"How do you know that?" I asked.

And he answered, "I know I have the clap! I'm going to see Doc Hartman."

I said, "You can't go see him at two in the morning! He'll throw you in the guard house!" and he retorted, "No, I'm going to see Doc Hartman. I'm going to see him, I've got the clap!"

Then he stormed out, down towards the officers and rousted Doc Hartman who, of course, sent him back to the hut until morning. Doc Hartman had a good sense of humor. Nothing was said about it, but this was one funny interlude in our lives.

Among my friends and crewmates, the only relationships we talked about were the casual ones. The guys who had steady relationships in and around the area didn't talk about them much, if any. We knew Mabry had a relationship with somebody because he was gone almost every night until the early morning hours. Euhas had a steady girl, and so did I—eventually—and none of us talked about them. We only talked about the casual one-night stands in London or in Norwich.

It rained most of the time that fall, but the few days when it cleared up and we didn't fly were just marvelous. The fields were golden, the trees had turned many colors, and the farmers were harvesting and piling up haystacks. I remember some glorious days when the sun drove the fog back out over the Channel and our crew was on stand-down (not scheduled for a mission). I was free to wander, so I would grab a bike and ride off, following the narrow, twisting country roads wherever they led.

In the villages and towns, the locals would wave. I would see women sweeping the stairs with big straw brooms like the kind witches fly on. I might stop to tease the swans and geese swimming in the pond in the center of Attleborough. I might pay a visit to the storekeeper with nothing to sell. He would ask, "How's England treating you, Yank?" All the time I was hoping to spot somebody whom I would like, somebody who would like me. I had some momentary romantic interludes which—believe me—helped a great deal.

The Cold Blue Sky

I remember one ride when I caught up with three English girls on bicycles. They wore the blue uniforms of the R.A.F. I rode along with them, laughing and joking. We stopped at a canteen for tea. One of them, an adorable girl, said goodbye to her friends, took me by the hand, and led me to an isolated pasture for some wonderful spontaneous love which we both seemed to need badly. Afterward, we parted with a casual goodbye and a promise to meet again. But in those days, promises were just words.

Then I rode on, stopping at an old Norman church that dated back to the thirteenth century and was still holding services. In the churchyard, old gravestones with illegible inscriptions lay tumbled upon each other. For a moment, standing there, I had a sense of past, present, and future. But then it was back to Snetterton Heath and our reality, the war, where only the present existed.

My favorite entertainment, if I got a pass to London, was to buy tickets to a play, hopefully meet somebody, spend the evening with her, and come home again. There was the time we were placed on stand-down for a couple of days and given a two-day pass to London. When we got to Victoria Station, we split up. It was a really pretty fall day. I walked over to Knightsbridge, booked myself a room at the N.C.O. Club where I always stayed, left my gear, walked over to nearby Hyde Park, and sat down on one of the benches. An older man in uniform came by, a veteran of World War One. He had a ticket machine like a conductor on a streetcar. I didn't know it at the time, but you had to buy an inexpensive ticket to sit there. I thought it was outrageous, but—what the hell—I gave him his halfpence.

I was resting by a body of water called the Serpentine, watching the ducks and the birds landing and the people walking by, and I noticed one girl in particular. She was walking with a G.I., an American infantry private, and they came by and said hello to me and asked if they could sit down. The ticket seller came back and collected a halfpence from each one of them. They had obviously sat there before and paid without protest. I commented that I'd never heard of being charged for sitting down on a bench.

The girl was very pretty, and best of all, they seemed more like friends than boyfriend and girlfriend. They said they had met about a month ago. Tom was at some training camp waiting for the invasion of France. Her name, if I remember, was Sandra. We talked for a while, and then he said he had to leave to meet somebody. After making arrangements to meet him again that evening, she stayed on with me.

We sat on the bench and talked. She told me her father was a major serving in North Africa. They lived in a two-flat building in a lower-end area known as Hammersmith; they had been bombed out of their home in a better area of London and had had to take what was available. Her maternal grandmother lived out in the country, and occasionally they would go out and stay with her when London was being heavily bombed. Her mother was a volunteer with the Women's Army Corps. Sandra was just finishing high school. She was going to be eighteen and was slated to go into the W.R.E.N.S., the women's naval auxiliary service, to do whatever had to be done, clerical work or whatever.

She said it was very difficult to date at that time and that Tom was the first American she had met and I was the second. Her father, she said, would probably throw a fit if he knew that she was talking with an American, especially one in what she called the "other ranks," with her father being an officer. I was a little more tolerable because I was a non-commissioned officer, but she said her father probably would have cut Tom in half, since Tom was only a private.

As usual on arriving in London, I had bought myself two tickets for a play that evening. I wasn't sure where Tom stood, but I asked if she would go with me, and she said she'd be happy to. She had brought some sandwiches with her, and we spread some napkins. It was some kind of chicken sandwich with very little chicken in it on a very mealy rye bread. I didn't particularly like the sandwich, but I was hungry and we shared it. She also had a hard-boiled egg, something I never liked, but I shared that with her too, and it turned out to be the best part of the meal, the hard-boiled egg with some salt she had brought along.

Then we went to a little tea house and then we walked over to the corner of Hyde Park to wait for Tom. He finally showed up with a young lady who was also a friend of Sandra's. They had other plans, and we decided to split up. I was going to take Sandra to the play. But until the play started at eight, we had no place to go. I couldn't take her back to my hotel. I was staying in a room with about ten bunks to house the guys who were spending the night. There was no way you get a woman in there. It wasn't allowed. So we went back to Hyde Park. It was getting dark, and we snuggled up on one of the benches, holding and kissing each other and talking. We didn't talk about what I was doing; instead, we talked about her plans after the war and how she would love to go to America after the war was over.

I admit it, any time a girl started talking like that, I would get a little edgy. It was as if I was only a ticket out of war-ravaged England —at this time, an extremely difficult place for civilians to live. They were on very short rations. Most of the men were away in other parts of the world fighting the war. Life was really hard for the people left behind. Added to all this, the bombing and destruction were far from over.

After a while, Sandra and I walked over to the U.S.O. at Piccadilly Circus. There you could get cocoa and tea, but no beer or hard drinks. It was so crowded, and so many people were milling about, that we decided to go back towards the other end of Piccadilly where the play was. By now it was getting close to show time. We went into the theater, handed over our tickets, and sat down in the relative comfort inside. These little theaters were beautiful with all the intricate gilding, plush seating, beautiful brocade curtains, and chandeliers. It was delightful—especially compared to my Nissen hut. I don't remember the play we saw that night, but I remember being very pleased to sit holding hands with this pretty girl.

When we got out of the play at about 10:00 or 10:30, we tried to find a place to get something to eat and drink, but it was impossible. Every place we walked to was just jammed, so we decided to stop by the U.S.O. again. There we grabbed ourselves a doughnut and more tea. Sandra had to get home, but the subways had already stopped running. When I asked how far it was, she said it would take about an hour to walk there. So I said, "Let's walk."

We walked and talked and held hands and kissed. I was really smitten with her. Walking in the blackout, hardly able to see in front of us, I relied on her to know where we were going. This was a wonderful interlude in my war, but I was frustrated that there was nowhere we could be alone that would be comfortable. Even as a young boy back in Chicago, all my friends had apartments and places of privacy where we could visit each other or listen to the radio. Both of us were feeling very young and amorous, but we didn't want to be crude about lovemaking. There was no place where we could be comfortable and let our feelings take over and hold each other and love each other.

We finally got to her door. You could hardly see the building because everything was black. The building was dark gray, the night was dark gray. I gave her my address so she could write to me and she gave me her address and we promised to get together again. I left her and started to walk back. It took me about an hour and a half to get back to Knightsbridge and it was after one in the morning when I got to sleep, feeling extremely frustrated.

About two weeks later, I got a card in the mail with an imprint of lipstick on it from Sandra. She wrote that she was very happy to have met me and asked why I hadn't written and whether she would be able to see me again. But at this time in my life, I did not think about the future. I had created for myself a day-to-day existence with absolutely no thought of any future. And I had found a local girlfriend.

Margot was twenty-six years old, seven years older than I. She lived about a mile from the base in a little cottage she shared with her two daughters, ages two and four.

I met Margot one day while I was out riding my bike. She was in her garden, and she looked over and smiled at me. I said hello and stopped to talk to her. She knew by my flight jacket that I was an airman. She told me her husband was an R.A.F. sergeant, a navigator in Lancaster bombers, and had been missing in action for over a year.

She invited me into her cottage. I'd only been in one English home prior to that, and it—unlike this one—was large. The rooms in Margot's house were surprisingly small and the ceilings low. It was an old cottage, probably dating back to the seventeenth or eighteenth century. Her children were in school, Margot told me. The younger one was with her sister-in-law, who also had some children and whose husband also flew in Lancasters. She showed me photographs of her children and one of her husband. I had to leave because we were scheduled for an afternoon practice mission. I said goodbye and asked if I could come back. She replied that she would like very much to see me again. I rode back to the base, which was only ten or fifteen minutes away.

The Cold Blue Sky

That same day we flew a practice mission. We did this quite often in those days, with Colonel Old up there in his plywood Mosquito or a P-47 barking orders, critiquing our formation flying. But we didn't mind. This was all part of our game plan to stay alive.

I was soon stopping by at Margot's every chance I had. I met her two delightful dark-haired little girls. Margot was also dark-haired. She almost looked Italian, but she spoke with a very nice, middle-class British accent. And before I knew it, we became lovers. I was very young and had a lot to learn about women. Margot turned out to be the most beautiful teacher I could have imagined.

Margot had a wonderful fragrance about her skin that I still remember. One thing about making love to Margot was that she would faint—literally pass out—during the sex act. This was both very gratifying to me and a little scary because I thought, "Wow! What a lover! I have the power of giving her so much pleasure that she passes out!" Either that or something was wrong with her. Whatever the case, lovemaking with Margot was a very exciting experience.

I loved the hours I spent with her, and not just for the sex. I liked the sensations of being in her cluttered little home. There was usually the smell of bread baking. I enjoyed just sitting down with her, having a cup of tea, and talking. She was a very understanding woman. She was bright and read a lot, as I did. She would give me a book which I would share with her. It became a lovely relationship. It was great having a lover and a friend so close to the air base—a refuge where I could have a change of attitude and scenery and escape from the war for brief periods.

Another good thing about having a friend like Margot was that her bathing facilities, though old-fashioned compared to what we had back in the States, were far superior to those on our base. So I enjoyed going to Margot's and taking a bath. It was luxurious.

Sometimes I would bring a can of fruit cocktail and a piece of cheese and some bread from the base. Our rations weren't that great, so I didn't have too much to take her. I knew a cook who would sometimes give me some butter to supplement her meager rations. But usually we'd have some toast and coffee that I'd managed to bring, and of course I'd bring some candy bars and chewing gum for the kids. It became scary for me in a way when the kids started calling me "Daddy." I don't know if she put them up to it, but she didn't correct them, and that bothered me.

She told me our affair was very difficult for her, because she was so fond of me. (We didn't dare talk of love then.) From where she lived, she was almost underneath the flight pattern of our base, and she could hear the planes taking off for a mission and watch them coming back. If, after a mission, I didn't visit her that night, she would be afraid that something had happened to me.

We talked about her school days and how she had met her husband at a village social. She appreciated the fact that I was risking my life on a routine basis just as her husband had. Later, other friends of mine and I found out that many of the local people had made a habit of counting the airplanes leaving the base and then counting those coming back. They knew as soon as we did how many we'd lost.

★   ★   ★

It was now October 1943—what we would later call Bloody October, the worst month of the Eighth Air Force's air war over Europe. It was a test of our endurance, of overcoming our fears. I'm proud to have taken part in Bloody October. To me, it was a great military feat—like the Charge of the Light Brigade, except that our attacks were more successful than the Light Brigade's.

We were starting to fly our missions as lead crew. I don't know if it was because we were better than the others or because we were one of the few remaining experienced crews. We definitely had a first-rate pilot, James Tolbert; maybe that's why they picked us.

I remember the night of October 4, when we were watching a World War One movie in our hut. On the screen the artillery was blasting away. All of a sudden, I punched Kelley on the shoulder said, "Jesus, this is realistic. Look, the hut is shaking!" We all ran outside.

German bombers were attacking our base. The 96th Bomb Group had twice as many planes and crews as other groups, so we were an attractive target. The sky was lit up by searchlights, and anti-aircraft guns boomed away in staccato. We went to our air-raid shelters. I crawled into one, but it was so claustrophobic that I decided to take my chances in the open. I sat outside and watched the air battle take place. It was unusual to be on the receiving end of it. I watched as the searchlights caught one of the intruders and anti-aircraft guns blew it out of the sky.

The Germans were growing adept at using radar, and the accuracy of their radar-aimed flak guns was rapidly increasing. Also, radar enabled German fighters to zero in on our bomber formations even when there was heavy cloud cover. For our October 8 mission to Bremen, we were issued huge, lightweight bags stuffed with narrow strips of aluminum foil (codenamed "Window" then and called "chaff" by later military generations). We were to open the bags and scatter these strips as we came over the target to interfere with German radar. Radar waves would bounce off the strips instead of our planes, so German radar wouldn't show where we were.

The Bremen mission was a rough one. The target was heavily defended by a great many anti-aircraft guns, and fighters attacked us before and after we reached the target. But the ruse with the aluminum chaff worked. It was quite a sight to see all these tons of aluminum foil shining in the sun, going down. It was even better to see the confused German fire. Our 96th Bomb Group was one of the few that had been issued this chaff. It must have helped, because we lost only three bombers that day while the 100th, who didn't use it, lost seven.

We got back to base with only a moderate amount of damage to the *Black Hawk*—just some holes in the wing and the tail section. No one in our plane was seriously hurt. I don't have the slightest idea whether any of us shot down any enemy aircraft on this mission. I know that we saw many German fighter planes explode as they swooped toward us, but who knows whether we or the gunners in another bomber got them. With many guns from several B-17s coming to bear on these enemy fighters, it was almost impossible to tell. None of our crew even bothered to claim kills any more, even though we all might have been aces by this time without knowing it. I often saw results that certainly seemed to be from my guns.

The next morning, October 9, we were roused at 0300 hours and went to briefing at 0500. When the curtain on the map was pulled back, all the crews started to moan and groan. The ribbon stretched across Denmark into the Baltic Sea, continued off the coast of Sweden, and made a right turn to the Polish port of Gdynia, not far from Danzig (now Gdánsk). In Gdynia we were going to bomb German naval installations and dock areas, any ships we found there, and possibly the Gestapo headquarters there. This was going to be one long, exhausting mission—eleven hours round trip.

The Gdynia mission is burned into my memory. We took off in the blackness before dawn, heavily loaded with extra fuel for a long mission. Dominic, the other waist gunner, and I hunkered down and held on while the *Black Hawk* roared down the runway. More Fortresses followed, one after the other, their exhausts spitting bursts of flames. We pulled up into the sky, barely missing the trees. A blast lit up the sky just ahead, and up we went through the heat and glare of what had been another B-17 just seconds ago. I found out something about myself then: I could still function despite the intense fear.

Our group was flying lead in the wing's box formation. The 388th flew low, and the high group was composed of planes from various other groups. Our formation was led by our new group commander, Lieutenant Colonel Jim Travis. We had no fighter escort at all, not even Spitfires. Our route took us on a wide approach over the North Sea, well offshore from Holland and Germany, then across the Danish coast and over lovely farmland neatly bordered by fences, hedges, and roads. From our altitude I couldn't see the cows or any details, but I could imagine serene rural scenes. Somewhere below, all that wonderful Danish butter was being produced for the German Army. I found myself thinking of cows and heavy cream.

We flew out over the Baltic, shivering from the bitter cold. Looking out to our right, we could see the coast of Germany. To our left we had a fantastic view of Sweden's magnificent broad beaches. Suddenly I saw a plane peel out of a formation up ahead and make a long coasting glide down onto one of the beaches. It didn't seem to have any mechanical problems. Maybe its crew decided to take a Swedish vacation from the rest of the war. I occasionally heard rumors about crews who defected to Switzerland or Sweden to get out of the war. In the early 1990s I saw a television documentary about it called "Whispers in the Air." But maybe somebody aboard was dying and needed immediate medical attention. Or maybe they had a mechanical problem. I never learned what really happened, but I couldn't judge them too harshly.

On and on we flew. Since we were over water, we attracted no flak, and for some reason we had yet to see any fighter opposition. But the cold was fearful. Every couple of minutes, we had to free our oxygen masks from ice by squeezing and draining the little bulb at the bottom where the spittle from our mouths collected and froze; otherwise, our masks would plug up. We had to remember to do that even in the heat of combat. Sometimes a guy would forget, and he would collapse. We would try to get to him before he died from lack of oxygen.

I was looking out for the enemy and admiring the scenery when Dominic punched my back to get my attention. I turned, and he was pointing to his parachute pack. I could see that both the harness he wore and his chute had solid steel rings. The chute should have had snaps to attach to the rings on the harness. Someone had made a mistake. As it was, his gear was useless. What a predicament! We had been told there was almost a thirty percent chance of having to bail out. I told him not to worry, that he could hold on to me if we had to jump. He took his mask off for a second, wiped his face, and gave me a sick grin. Fortunately for both of us, we didn't have to bail out, because I don't think we would have made it.

We flew beyond the prewar border between Germany and Poland and made a right turn around the Bay of Danzig. Before we knew it, we were over Gdynia. The whole harbor was covered with smoke. They must have known we were coming, because they had lit smoke pots to obscure the target. Through the smoke we could see a German pocket battleship being towed out of the harbor. Our group started to make a bomb run on the battleship, but as we were coming over the target, the clouds obscured it. Colonel Travis led us around in a big circle for a second bomb run. The anti-aircraft fire was intense. Every ship of war that the Germans had plus all the rest of the anti-aircraft guns were shooting at us. The pocket battleships and cruisers could aim 155-mm guns at us, and if one of those shells exploded within half a block of you, it would shake you like a rat in a cat's mouth.

On our second bomb run we hit one of the German cruisers as well as the former luxury liner *Stuttgart,* and then we bombed most of the port facilities. Somebody got a direct hit on Gestapo headquarters. We heard at a later date through the Polish Underground that the bomb destroyed a great many records and thereby saved the lives of people who would have been future victims of the Gestapo. Several prisoners being held for execution escaped during the bombing. We also killed a fair number of Gestapo agents that day. That was a very gratifying thing to do. For the first time, I felt that our bombing was worthwhile. I was proud that we were strict about not bombing civilian targets but went after isolated naval targets and specifically dock areas where the navy ships were.

After our second turn around the target area, we came back through intense anti-aircraft fire, reached the Baltic again, and headed for home. As we were flying down the Baltic, I saw a JU-88 about 2,000 yards away flying parallel to us. Dominic, the other gunner, came over as I decided to take a couple of pot shots at it. Dominic corrected my aim and I raised my gun a little and fired a blast corrected by tracers. I saw pieces fly off this JU-88. The pilot banked and moved another thousand yards away. Just then, Tolbert said on the intercom, "Hold off on the fire! Save your ammunition!"

Never were truer words spoken. In about ten minutes we were under attack by a minimum of a hundred German FWs, ME-109s, and JU-88s. They buzzed around our group's forty-six Fortresses like angry hornets, attacking from every angle and every altitude. Some fired rockets, which exploded with a much bigger bang than flak. I saw six enemy fighters coming directly at my left waist position with their guns blazing away. I kept breaking from one plane to another, going back and forth, firing with short bursts. The radio (top turret) gunner couldn't get his gun down far enough to bring them into his sights. The tail gunner was totally occupied. Then the fighters swooped past, and we were unhit. How they missed I still cannot fathom.

At one time our lead squadron was under attack by about fifty German fighters. Our navigator yelled out on the intercom that German planes were dragging bombs on cables. This was a new tactic. You could see the light reflected off these bombs being carried on cables by Heinkel bombers flying above our formation and in the opposite direction. The Germans were dragging the bombs right through our formation. One bomb caught the plane on our right and blew it up. The force of the explosion knocked the *Black Hawk* up and over on its back. Then the plane plunged thousands of feet downward—5,000, maybe 10,000 feet in all. Dominic and I were thrown against the door leading to the radio hatch. Down we went, pulling all the wiring and the oxygen tubes away from our heads. Everything loose, including ammo boxes and parachutes, piled up against us. Spent shell casings flew around in the fuselage like marbles in a tin bucket.

We usually didn't wear our parachutes because the big chest-pack chutes were too bulky and impeded our movements. Mine always seemed to be in the way when I wore it. I kept it stowed right beside me where I could grab it. But now, as the *Black Hawk* went into its dive, I didn't have my parachute.

I didn't feel any panic. I just tried to move my arms, but they were pinned by gravity to the radio room door. Suddenly our plane leveled out, although it was shaking like a tin roof in a hurricane. I grabbed my parachute, pushed the ammo boxes off me, and made my way to the waist compartment. On our waist door we had a little handle with an explosive charge to open it. I blew the door off and I was ready to go, with no second thoughts.

I looked down and saw the North Sea, but I didn't even think about the fact that I couldn't swim. I just thought that getting out of the plane would give me a second chance. As I was going out, somebody grabbed my shoulder. It was Dominic. Then I remembered: He had no chute, or no chute that would work, and I'd promised to jump with him. I turned around and there was Jimmy Spell, opening the radio door. He was waving at us to come in, that we were all right. Back we went and reconnected our oxygen masks and heated suits. The plane was shuddering like hell. It was a terrible mess inside, but we managed to regain our formation, and on we flew.

That was as dramatic a moment as any in my combat career. I was a split second from leaping out into the icy North Sea. In that moment when I was poised to jump, I knew that even if I survived the jump, I would have to untangle my parachute so I would not drown, then inflate my life vest and stay afloat. Not knowing how to swim, hoping to be picked up in the next twenty minutes, I was very aware that hypothermia from the cold North Sea water would kill me in less than half an hour. Needless to say, I'm glad I didn't jump.

We regained altitude and rejoined the formation. As we were flying along, another B-17 took up a position alongside us and started flying formation in place of the one that had gone down. On our way across Denmark, I noticed that this plane now had two engines smoking. The crew started dumping their ammo boxes and anything else that could lighten their load. They even started to drop some of their extra machine guns. Even so, they began to fall back out of formation. I looked at this other waist gunner who was busy dumping stuff out of the plane, and he looked at me, and I tried to signal him that I wished I had a rope that I could tie to him and help him. He just kind of looked at me and gave me a thumbs up, and they fell away and that's the last we ever saw of them. I kept trying to lift them with my arm as they disappeared behind us.

We were still under enemy air attack. After reconnecting all my equipment, I reached for my gun and started blazing away again. This air battle continued for about an hour and a half. If a Fortress fell behind, another one took its place. With the formation tight, the gunners alert, and the fire accurate, with the pilots flying well and keeping all possible guns bearing on an approaching enemy, shifting position if we were attacked from another side, we were a formidable adversary for the German fighters.

The 96th avoided a catastrophe that day thanks to the skill of our pilots and the hard training we'd received from our former commander, Colonel Old. He was a tremendous leader.

The Gdynia mission still wasn't over. Something had happened to my heater wiring during all the tossing around. I was looking out my left waist window for enemy fighters when Dominic punched me on the back and pointed to my right foot. Smoke was pouring from my boot. While we were staring at it, my foot blazed into flame. Without hesitating, Dominic pulled out his penis. It took a minute to find it under all his clothes. He proceeded to pee on my foot, putting out the fire. I slapped him on the back for his ingenuity and turned back to my gun.

Finally we left the Danish coast behind, and the German fighters abandoned their pursuit. We flew on toward England, getting low on gasoline. It got darker and the formation broke up because of the danger of collision. We were used to daylight returns, so it was eerie coming back to England as night engulfed us. We found ourselves alone in the black sky.

Approaching the English coast, Tolbert called "Mayday" on the radio because we were running out of gas. Then he gave the coded call asking for guidance: "Darkey, darkey, where are you?" As we crossed the coast, two searchlights came on. This was the first I'd seen of the system used for the R.A.F. night bombers when they came back from their missions. We lined up on the searchlights, and as we approached they went out and two more came on farther away. This continued all the way across England. The searchlights kept coming on, and we flew down the path that they marked.

The lights guided us back to East Anglia; then we were on our own. We made our approach to an airfield, but at the last minute Tolbert realized it wasn't our field but that of the 100th. We flew on, sighted the large manor house at Snetterton Heath in the moonlight, and finally made a safe landing at our own field. My misadventures continued, however. When we parked, Doc Hartman and a medic came over to look at my foot. They cut my boot away, then looked at me with disgust. My foot was encased in frozen urine. It was frostbitten and burned at the same time. I could hardly walk, but I refused to let them put me on a stretcher, take me to the hospital, or prevent me from flying.

I wasn't so worried about my foot. I was worried about how my family would react to news of my wound—my brother, who was in the Army in Washington State; my father; and most of all, my mother. I knew that if something serious happened to me, the youngest, they would all be devastated. I had no idea how they were taking my being in air combat, or how the papers were describing the air raids. I didn't even know if the air raids were making it into the papers. To tell the truth, my family didn't learn I was flying combat until I was wounded the first time—the shrapnel in the stomach on the Kassell mission. Then they received a telegram stating only that I'd been wounded in action and that details would follow. This was enough to give anyone a heart attack. They were hysterical until I was able to write that I had survived and was well enough to go back on duty.

In spite of my protests, I was given another medal for my frozen foot: an oak leaf cluster for the Purple Heart I already had. I didn't want it because my mother would receive another telegram. I didn't want her to worry unnecessarily. But it was no use; they gave it to me anyway.

The next morning, October 10, we dragged ourselves out of our bunks to be briefed for another major mission. Our target was the railroad yards and junctions of Münster, a city in northwestern Germany. Our I.P.—the initial point, not the target—was the huge cathedral, which we were told was the premier cathedral in all of Germany. Münster was our first primarily civilian target. Some of the crew members objected that we were going to hit a church town on a Sunday. It was a major transportation and shipping point, but it was still primarily a civilian target.

We felt uneasy about this. We had been in London when the Germans raided it and had seen damage in most parts of England, where the Germans seemed to have bombed indiscriminately. We knew about the German bombing of the English cathedral city of Coventry and the Dutch city of Rotterdam. We knew about the destruction of Warsaw, the Polish capital. We knew how indiscriminate and cruel the Nazis had been in their bombing, and yet we were reluctant to go against this city.

At that time I did not know about the planned destruction of whole races of people—the Jews, the Gypsies, the "misfits"— which was going on in concentration camps in Germany and Poland. I knew that Jews were being mistreated, that they had to wear yellow stars, that they were being locked up and beaten up but I did not know of the genocide at this time. If I had known, I probably would have volunteered, like Hubner, for whatever destructive mission I could go on against Germany.

This was the third straight day we had to fly a major mission. So many planes had been damaged that our 96th Bomb Group could put only twenty-one B-17s in the air—of which three had to turn back. Our group was in high formation, following the 100th, the 385th and the 95th. Due to their limited range, our P-47 fighter escort had to turn back just beyond the German frontier. Shortly before reaching Münster, we were hit by an intense fighter attack. Some of the participants say that this was our fiercest air battle of the war. From our high position we could look out and watch the groups ahead of us being chopped to pieces. Of the twelve Fortresses which the 100th Bomb Group put over the target, only two came back, and one of those was damaged beyond repair. The rest were shot down by flak or by fighters. Somehow, our group lost only one bomber and crew that day. But other groups were badly mauled. In all, thirty U.S. bombers were shot down. The Münster raid came to be called "Black Sunday."

One story is that the 100th Bomb Group was singled out for destruction because, on a previous mission, one of its planes was in trouble and it had dropped out of formation and lowered its landing wheels, which was the sign of surrender. As the German fighters had swarmed around it to escort it to a base, the gunners opened fire and shot down several of the German planes. The Luftwaffe fighter pilots vowed revenge on any formation of B-17s showing a square with a D on their tails. Our group's insignia was a square with a C.

I often wondered about the luck of the draw on Münster and other missions, where we watched Fortresses going down all around us with the target yet to be reached. The flashing cannons of German fighters and the flak guns flickering all around the landscape below were aimed at us. Shrapnel was raining off the thin aluminum skin of our B-17. Yet our *Black Hawk* plunged on through.

When we got back to the base, several of our aircraft had major damage but, other than the crew of the missing plane, so far as I know no one else in our bomb group was hurt that day. We went to debriefing and described how we had watched the devastation of the groups ahead of us. We didn't know yet how many planes were actually lost. Sometimes we suffered a major disaster and weren't aware of it right away. But this time we had seen the planes blowing up and debris scattered all along the ground.

That evening, after I'd had a cup of coffee, I decided to leave my bike and walk to Margot's cottage through the fog and rain. The walk didn't take more than half an hour. I walked along the railroad past the boundary of the base and then cut across the fields, which had a lot of undergrowth and many stunted, leafless trees growing close together. Margot was happy to see me.

We were still on alert, so I had to get back to base by 0200. It was very foggy when I left Margot's. Coming back over the fields and along the railroad tracks with the fog swirling and only a sliver of moonlight to cast slight shadows, I thought of Sherlock Holmes and the Hound of the Baskervilles. The fields became alive. The tree limbs moved and seemed to grab at me. I became so frightened that I started to run. I tripped once and got up and ran faster. The more I ran, the more panicky I got.

Finally, I got close to the flight line and I could hear the putt-putt of the little engines of the maintenance vehicles. The noise told me that the ground crews were getting us ready for another mission. For once it was very gratifying to hear those sounds of life, because I really got myself terrified on that walk home.

Chapter Nine

A major raid was coming up, and somehow we guessed it was Schweinfurt. The last Eighth Air Force mission to Schweinfurt had been devastating for both sides. We had flown the diversionary raid to Regensburg on that deadly day in August. We knew what a dangerous target Schweinfurt was. Sure enough, early in October we were alerted for a second mission to Schweinfurt. But the alert was canceled, and we stood down.

I was walking across the base and saw a group of officers —Colonel Old, Colonel Travis, and a couple of squadron leaders—escorting Adolphe Menjou, the movie actor, looking distinguished in a combat jacket. Menjou nodded to me as they walked by. I was thrilled.

One evening Spell, Dutch, Hunt and I grabbed a ride on an Army truck for the half-hour trip into Norwich. We had decided to go to the Hotel Norwich to get something decent to eat, so we were all washed up and clean when we walked into the hotel's elegant dining room. We looked at the menu and the only meat we could find was rabbit. Hunt looked over and said, "I'm going to have this. I never could eat it before but I want it." He showed me the item on the menu and there it was, or so I thought—Welsh Rabbit. I looked at it and said, "Shit!"

When I was growing up, I used to see rabbits in the Polish butcher shops in my neighborhood, and I thought I could never eat one. But I was so hungry for fresh meat that I decided to try it. When it was served, Hunt and I were aghast. There was no rabbit. There was only melted cheese over toast with tomato slices. We called the waiter over and asked him, "Where's the rabbit?" He said, "It's there!" Well, after a good deal of back and forth, we found out that Welsh *Rabbit* was *Rarebit,* and it was no rabbit, just a glorified grilled cheese sandwich! So much for our meat dish and so much for our education in cosmopolitan dining.

After dinner we took a walk in the total blackout and looked for a movie house. We carried a flashlight, and I shined the beam across the street to look at the theater marquee to see what was playing. All of a sudden, a voice piped up: "You bloody Yanks, put that light out!" It was an English bobby. This was a pretty stupid thing for me to do because one little light could tip off a German fighter-bomber pilot that he was over the city.

We stopped at a pub. The other guys had a beer and I had a little glass of port. We sat there killing time, talking, and waiting for the truck's pick-up time, around 2300 hours. But we became restless, so we caught a bus back to Snetterton Heath. When we arrived, the base hummed with activity. Around every plane were ground crews working under shielded lights. Planes that had been half-cannibalized for parts were being reassembled. Something big was coming down. We instinctively knew where we were going to go tomorrow: Schweinfurt.

An icy fear enveloped me. I turned into a robot. Everything else vanished from my mind. In our hut no one said a word. I climbed into my top bunk and stared at the ceiling. I was frightened to death, but there was nobody to talk to. My mind raced. How could I get out of it? But I didn't want to get out of it. I couldn't let my fellow crew members down. Anyway, there was nothing I could do about any of it.

We were probably all praying silently for tomorrow's weather to be so bad that we wouldn't have to go. But we also knew that eventually we would have to go, so our prayers probably changed to wanting to get it over with. It was just a mess of conflicting emotions for us all.

Once in a while, we heard about a pilot or gunner going to the operations officer and demanding to be taken off flying status. They didn't want to fly any more; they didn't care what was done with them, they just wouldn't fly. But that didn't happen often.

I remember one case where a returning gunner remained in the waist of the plane, cowering and whimpering. There was nothing wrong with him. He hadn't been shot, he wasn't frozen, and his color was good, so we knew he didn't suffer from lack of oxygen. He just lay on the floor, curled up like a small baby, crying and whimpering and refusing to talk. They carried him off in a stretcher. We never saw or heard of him again. And nobody on the crew could explain what happened. Obviously the poor guy was just frightened to death.

I immediately understood his fear, but I also knew I could never do what he did. When I thought about the missions I still had to fly, something in my makeup said, "Do it! Go through it!" I had to. I couldn't have lived with myself if I had quit. I thought it was better to die in combat than to destroy my name.

I finally managed to close my eyes and doze a little bit. About an hour later I was awakened by the Charge of Quarters, opening doors and shouting, "Up and at 'em! Up and at 'em!" This time he was waking everyone. All the crews, even those who weren't scheduled for the mission, were going to fly as spares in case mechanical problems forced some planes to turn back.

We dressed and marched through the cold rain to the mess hall. They were serving fresh eggs—another indication of a dangerous mission. For some reason they felt better if they gave us fresh eggs. Perhaps we'd be more willing to die after a good breakfast. But the eggs were welcome to some of the guys. I didn't like eggs much, so it didn't make any difference to me. I managed to get a cup of coffee down. I was almost like a zombie with fear. I walked to the briefing on wooden legs.

Everyone was crowded into the briefing room, including the doctors and chaplains. When Colonel Old came in, everybody stood at attention. The intelligence officer uncovered the map, and there it was, a ribbon leading deep into Germany to Schweinfurt, some sixty miles east of Frankfurt. We had known in our guts that Schweinfurt would be the target; still, it was a shock to see it up there.

Then an officer read a telegram from General Fred L. Anderson of Eighth Bomber Command:

SECRET.

TO ALL LEADERS AND COMBAT CREWS. TO BE READ AT BRIEFING.

THIS AIR OPERATION TODAY IS THE MOST IMPORTANT AIR OPERATION YET CONDUCTED IN THIS WAR. THE TARGET MUST BE DESTROYED. IT IS OF VITAL IMPORTANCE TO THE ENEMY. YOUR FRIENDS AND COMRADES THAT HAVE BEEN LOST AND THAT WILL BE LOST TODAY ARE DEPENDING ON YOU. THEIR SACRIFICE MUST

NOT BE IN VAIN. GOOD LUCK, GOOD SHOOTING, AND GOOD BOMBING.

ANDERSON

On hearing the closing, "Good luck, good shooting, and good bombing," some crews yelled, "And goodbye!"

Colonel Old got up and said, "Men, this has to be done." He told us the whole German air force and army rode on ball bearings, and he said if we could destroy the Schweinfurt ball bearing factories, we would set the German war effort back to the Stone Age. He called it the most important mission to date and probably one of the most important missions of the war. He also said that he would lead our 96th Bomb Group, which was going to lead the entire Third Division, a total of 154 B-17s. The Third Division would be thirty minutes behind Colonel Budd J. Peaslee's First Bomb Division, which was spearheading this massive attack by the Eighth Air Force.

Colonel Old would be in a highly vulnerable position in the lead plane, *Fertile Myrtle*. He would fly in the co-pilot's seat with Major Thomas F. Kenny as first pilot. The 96th was putting forty-one Fortresses into the air, divided into A and B Groups. Six of our crews flew planes borrowed from other bomb groups.

Our *Black Hawk* would lead the low squadron of B Group—also an unenviable position. German fighters tried to take out the leading bombers because these planes had the better and more experienced crews, and because shooting down the leaders would disrupt our formations. The remaining bombers would have to regroup, with other crews taking the places of the leaders. Aside from this, the low squadron itself was in a vulnerable position—especially on turns, when it was easy for the low squadron, trailing the others, to get left behind. All too often, German fighters were waiting to pounce.

A briefing officer said that fighter opposition would be extremely heavy; at least 1,200 German fighters were based along our route to Schweinfurt. Our P-47s would escort us as far as Emden, Germany, which is near the coast at the Dutch border. After that we would be on our own. We were told to expect extremely heavy flak on the way into the target. The weather over the target was expected to be clear, although the Germans would light a lot of smoke pots to obscure Schweinfurt with smoke. But some of our lead elements had radar, and we were told that we would bomb by radar if necessary.

The navigators, bombardiers, and pilots separated for individual briefings. Then we all reassembled, and Colonel Old read us another message—this one from Secretary of War Henry L. Stimson and Army Air Force Chief of Staff General Henry H. "Hap" Arnold. It said, "You who are about to die today will not have died in vain." I thought that was a hell of a stupid message, and I'm sure I wasn't the only one who thought so.

We went to the crew room for our parachutes and Mae West life jackets. The Catholic and Protestant guys went to see their respective chaplains, some kneeling for a blessing. One guy looked at me when I was at my locker and said he knew he wasn't going to make it. "Shit," I said, "You don't know that any more than I do, and I'm going to make it." I said this as much for my own reassurance as for his.

At the armorer's hut I took three gun barrels and requested several more boxes of ammunition than usual. As a crew, we normally carried 10,000 rounds of ammo. But that day we asked our pilot to take twice as much. This was an extraordinary request; ammunition was extremely heavy, and there was no use having extra if we couldn't get off the ground. We had seen too many overloaded planes crash on takeoff. Captain Tolbert agreed to take it. (His promotion, long overdue in his eyes, had recently come through.)

We grabbed our gear, hopped on a truck, and were dropped us off at the *Black Hawk's* hardstand beside the railroad tracks. The morning commuter train came by. Tolbert and Macleod walked around the plane, checking it out. Dominic and I stowed our guns and opened our windows. Each of us checked his ammo and threaded it into the container, then into the scoop which fed into the gun. We made sure the guns were on safety and stowed for take-off, then climbed out of the airplane for a last break. Some of the guys smoked. All of us answered the call of nature in our favorite row of Brussels sprouts, which by that time were getting monstrous. I wondered what the farmer thought about them.

As we waited in the drizzle, I didn't talk to anybody. I didn't even look at anybody. I was just trying to cope with my own private terror. Then a jeep drove up, and Colonel Old got out. He came over, looked us all in the eye, and talked to us for a moment, wishing us Godspeed and good luck. I thought to myself, "He's got guts. He's the commanding officer of the Bomb Wing, and he didn't have to fly, but he chose to lead this one."

Tolbert looked at his watch and said, "Let's get into the planes." Spell, the radio man, picked this moment to sing "Off We Go into the Wild Blue Yonder." We all climbed in and waited some more. It had been light since around 0600. About 1030 hours, up came the green flares. Our engines sputtered, pop-popped, then roared to life. Out of my left-side window I saw our ground crew chief, Johnny Euhas, holding his hat in the immense draft of the propellers and giving me the "thumbs up." He signaled to the pilot that everything was clear.

At the head of the low squadron, we taxied slowly behind Colonel Old and the lead squadron into take-off position. Right behind the other aircraft, Tolbert goosed the *Black Hawk*'s engines into full throttle, and we roared down the runway into a dreamy English sky. There we rendezvoused with the high group, headed toward The Wash, and circled while the others formed up behind us. Then we headed out over the North Sea.

Everyone was very quiet. There was no talk on the intercom except for the routine oxygen check when we reached 10,000 feet and the order to check our guns once we were out over the water. Pretty soon we could see puffs coming from all the airplanes as the gunners shot off a few rounds. Our plane shuddered as we squeezed off our trial shots.

I was having a conversation with myself. One side of me kept saying, "This is the day. You're really going to catch hell today. They're waiting for us. It's going to be the worst yet." The other side was saying, "It's just another mission. You've lived through more than half of them so far. Nothing is going to happen to you." Still, deep down, I thought the odds would eventually get me.

Over the North Sea our formation slowly gained altitude, giving the planes a chance to unkink any mechanical problems. To the rear I could see four more Fortresses from our 96th Bomb Group waiting to take over if somebody aborted.

I looked down at the water and saw seven huge whale-like shapes. I reported a squadron of submarines to the navigator, who made a note of it. Usually, if we saw anything important, we informed the navigator over the intercom, and he would put it on his time and latitude chart so that later it could be traced accurately. Radio silence prevented us from alerting the British anti-submarine command. Once we took off, there was no radio traffic between the aircraft and the ground. We communicated by shooting flares of various colors. The pilots could talk to each other, and the commander of the force could communicate with his pilots, but we did not communicate with the ground because the Germans could easily pick that up. When we bombed a target, the leader broke radio silence for a brief moment to send a strike signal back to England—for example, "Primary bombed."

On we flew, going higher and getting colder. In the ice-blue stratosphere where we leveled off, the temperature was sixty below zero Fahrenheit. I looked up and saw two groups of American P-47 fighters heading out to cover the First Bomb Division, which was leading the entire strike.

The major difference between this mission and the earlier ones was our knowledge and fear of Schweinfurt. Sure, we had survived some very tough missions. But this time the devil had a familiar face. We knew what a horribly rough time the First Bomb Division had had on its earlier strike against Schweinfurt. We felt sure that the Germans knew we were coming and that they had amassed a huge fighter ambush for us, in addition to lining the area with every conceivable flak gun they could find. We also knew that this might not be the last Schweinfurt mission. It might take several more tries to destroy the target.

I looked out my window and saw what appeared to be a division of sixty B-24s, American "Liberator" heavy bombers, about a thousand yards from us. As I watched, red flares suddenly shot from the lead plane, the pilot made a sharp turn, and the entire division turned and followed him back toward England.

Many years later, I read that only twenty-four of the sixty B-24s had managed to rendezvous, and Bomber Command decided to send this small force on a diversionary mission to the Frisian Islands in the North Sea, in hopes of luring some fighters away from us. At the time it appeared that the B-24s had aborted their mission, and it had a tremendous effect on us. Then we began to see some B-17s turning back. Why they were aborting, I don't know—maybe sickness, or mechanical problems, or fear.

We were originally going in with 377 bombers. Now we were down to around 290 B-17s, and still more of those would turn back with mechanical problems. Others would be shot down on the way in. Ultimately, only 227 would make it to the target. I didn't know the numbers at the time, but I knew lots of planes had turned back. It was clear that our force had been weakened. And we were heading for perhaps the most heavily-defended German airspace of all.

Even though I was frightened, I was so exhausted that I fell asleep standing up. I don't know if I slept two seconds or half an hour, but while I was asleep, I was in a safe, warm place, dreaming a delightful dream, and there was no war. Suddenly I was jolted back into harsh reality by the bombardier calling over the intercom that the fighter escort ahead of us was turning back. We hadn't even reached the German border yet. I felt completely abandoned. Now we were all alone.

Almost immediately, crew members reported enemy aircraft coming in at all positions. I was a teenager. I was scared. I wanted to live. I wondered how the hell I had ended up in this situation.

The navigator made a crew check to see that everybody had his oxygen on and that there were no problems. He called Dutch, the ball turret gunner, and couldn't make contact. So he called me and said, "Check Dutch." I disconnected my oxygen, put on my portable oxygen bottle—it had about seven or eight minutes of oxygen—and went to the ball turret. I pounded on the turret with my gloved hand as hard as I could. Dutch finally rotated the turret upwards. It was a great relief when I saw that turret move.

I popped the hatch and he looked up at me. I had to remove my oxygen mask and yell at him, "Dutch, what's the matter? We couldn't get hold of you." Just that simple act of communication was very difficult with the wind howling and the motors roaring. He finally understood, looked at his intercom, and saw it had been disconnected. He plugged it in and checked in with the navigator, and everything was okay. I put my oxygen mask back on, went back to my position, and plugged myself in again. The icy wind blew in through both waist gun openings, and I was back to freezing.

Most of the action was up ahead, where the German fighters were swarming around the planes of the First Division leading the strike. On we flew, watching the destruction of the Fortresses ahead of us. Stricken B-17s curved downward, trailing smoke. Here and there parachutes blossomed among the flak bursts—white chutes for the American bomber crews, yellow ones for the German fighter pilots. Finally, the last formation of the First Division completed their bomb run and turned away from the target area. It was our turn.

As we approached the target, we came under constant fighter attack from every imaginable position. My heart was pounding with both anxiety and exhilaration from the fierce combat. Between the flak explosions that buffeted us and the evasive action taken by our pilot, our plane felt like a cork in a typhoon. Everywhere I looked, B-17s were bucking all over the sky. Tossed from side to side, hardly able to stand, I was trying to shoot accurately—to hit the German fighters, not to shoot our wing off or riddle the B-17 next to us. I kept calling on the intercom to tell Tolbert to raise or lower the plane so that I could get clear shots, and he always responded quickly.

There was a terrific crash. I looked out and saw a huge hole in our right wing. It may have been just inches from the gas tank, but there was no smoke or fire, so on we went. Then I heard another bang, and I looked behind me, and there was a big hole in the tail section. I called Hunt, the tail gunner, on the intercom, but there was no answer. I couldn't do anything for a minute because we were under heavy attack from fighters as well as anti-aircraft fire. For once the German fighters were flying through their own flak. Usually they turned away when we came under anti-aircraft fire, because they were in just as much danger of being hit by flak as we were.

Tolbert stopped his evasive action, steadied the *Black Hawk* for our bomb run, and turned over control of the plane to the bombardier. We flew as straight and level as possible, still buffeted by the bursts of flak. The fighters had finally halted their attacks, so I went back to check on our tail gunner.

Hunt was lying nearly unconscious in his combat position. He hadn't been wounded, but his radio and oxygen equipment had been shot away. Dominic and I pulled him towards the waist compartment and gave him some oxygen from one of our masks. Hunt couldn't bend his feet at all; I figured they'd been frozen. He finally caught his breath and, gutsy guy that he was, dragged himself back to his tail position where he was able to hook his oxygen and his heated suit back up. We were quite vulnerable during the time he was away from his position. But now the stinger was back in our tail.

Finally, the bombardier yelled, "Bombs away!" and we turned away from the target area. Below us, thick black smoke boiled up from what we hoped were the ball bearing plants down below. We didn't want to have to come back.

As we turned away from the target area to form up again with our group and wing, I noticed a terrific banging up ahead in the plane. Spell called back, "One bomb didn't fall." We had a 500-pound bomb hanging from one shackle. The wind and the movement of the plane were banging it back and forth, and the little propeller on the back of the bomb was spinning in the breeze. Once a propeller made so many revolutions, the bomb would arm itself and would be ready to blow up on contact. That would be the end of the *Black Hawk*—and us.

On the intercom, I heard that Spell was going to put on a portable oxygen mask and try to kick the bomb loose from the shackle. The banging continued. Tolbert called and told me to go up front and check. Spell was unconscious—his portable bottle must have been out of oxygen—so I gave him a whiff of mine, and he revived right away. Then the two of us balanced ourselves on that narrow catwalk, which wasn't much over a foot wide at its widest point, and together we started to pound at that damned bomb. Its propeller was still going, and time was running out.

I tried to reach down and grab the prop to stop it from spinning, but it was too far away. Then I passed out. Spell revived me with the oxygen bottle. Then Spell passed out again, and I revived him. Finally, I managed to put one foot and some of my weight on the bomb while I wrapped my arms around the catwalk and hung on. The earth was five miles below. While I dangled there and pushed on the bomb with my foot, Spell gave a mighty kick. The bomb came loose and fell away. The bombardier could finally close the bomb bay doors, and we went back to our positions. Even now, so many years later, telling this story sets my heart pounding again.

While I was up helping Spell dispose of the bomb, Dominic had been running back and forth between my gun and his gun. Was he glad to see me when I got back! The fighting raged on—a continuous, running air battle all the way back into Holland. As we were approaching the North Sea, some P-47s appeared and gave us cover. By this time the 96th Bomb Group had lost about seven airplanes. We didn't know the extent of the damage the Eighth Air Force had suffered, but we knew it was considerable.

The Cold Blue Sky

On our way back across the Continent, the sky had been littered with exploding planes and parachutes, and we could see plumes of smoke where planes had crashed and burned.

Whether or not our crew shot down any fighters that day, I don't know. I don't think any of us knew, even though we saw lots of enemy aircraft blow up. I don't think anybody in the crew paid any attention any longer to who got what. We just kept up a God-awful return fire at anything in range with a swastika or a Luftwaffe cross on it.

We made it back to base, landed, and taxied to our strip. After surviving this harrowing mission unharmed, as I was exiting the plane I hit my head against a sharp piece of aluminum and put a deep gash in my forehead. I'm a big bleeder, and head wounds bleed a lot anyway. Before I knew it, my entire head was covered with blood. Two medics came running by with a stretcher, heading for a plane that had shot flares off to signal that it had wounded aboard. They took one look and detoured over to me, then tried to force me onto the stretcher. I yelled, "I'm not wounded! I just banged my head!" They kept trying to push me down, and I kept trying to get up, still yelling, "I'm not wounded!" Spell was standing there, laughing hysterically. Finally, I managed to make the medics understand that I had did not need emergency medical attention and that there were badly wounded guys in other planes waiting for them. They finally left me alone and took care of the badly wounded.

Soon we saw them carrying some of the wounded out of Colonel Old's plane. I didn't know it at this time, but Old himself had been hit by flak. Reportedly, he took a load of anti-aircraft shrapnel in the butt. The navigator was killed. The bombardier, badly wounded, still managed to drop the bombs.

Most of the crews quietly assessed each other on our way to briefing. Nobody was bragging. The guy from another crew who said to me before the mission that he wouldn't make it—well, he didn't.

I tried to wipe the blood off my face, but I still looked a mess. I even had blood in the creases at the corners of my eyes. I was only eighteen, but my face was nearly as deeply lined as it is today, and all those lines were full of blood. We were exhausted and yet exhilarated to be among the living. We knew that we had lost airplanes, but we hadn't heard the final count. Sometimes aircraft landed at other air bases and we'd hear later on. We went to briefing and there, one of the majors from intelligence came right out and said that the Eighth Air Force had lost a tremendous number of aircraft that day. Usually, they don't say anything of the sort.

After getting something to eat—bread, fruit cocktail, and coffee—I went back to the hut. That evening the infamous Lord Haw-Haw came on the Tannoy radio in our hut and read a German communiqué stating that the Luftwaffe had practically wiped out the remnants of the Eighth Air Force. The Germans claimed they had shot down 112 bombers. We didn't know whether it was true or not, but we couldn't dismiss the claim out of hand.

The aim of the German fighter defense was to wipe out the First Bomb Division, then turn against our Third Division and eliminate us. Fortunately, because of the courage and concentration of our B-17 crews and the fierce fire directed at enemy aircraft, that didn't happen. Still, it was bad enough—our heaviest losses ever, in our biggest air battle ever. The Eighth Air Force's official tally was that of the 291 B-17s sent to Schweinfurt, sixty were shot down, and seventy-five percent of the returning aircraft suffered severe damage. Some 600 American airmen were dead, wounded, or missing.

Colonel Peaslee's First Bomb Division led the Schweinfurt raid that day and suffered the most, with forty-five B-17s shot down. Our Third Division lost fifteen Fortresses—seven of them from our 96th Group's contingent of forty-one planes. The 96th brought many wounded back to the base, and most of the planes were damaged. Only about half a dozen planes from our group would have been able to fly if we'd had a mission the next day.

We examined our *Black Hawk* and found numerous small flak holes all over the aircraft, including many holes where 20-mm bullets had gone all the way through the plane. The big hole I had noticed in our wing turned out to be almost three and a half feet wide, and it missed the fuel tank by a scant half an inch. The one in the tail had almost blown the vertical stabilizer off. We came so close to being knocked out of the sky. It was a miracle we survived.

In the last four missions, the Eighth Air Force had seen nearly 150 of its bombers shot down and 1,500 of its men killed or taken prisoner. Yet here we were, still alive and still flying.

The Cold Blue Sky

That night I went back to the hut but couldn't sleep, so I got on a bike and rode over to Margot's place. I was grateful to have her home as a refuge. We went out for a quiet walk. There were no lights. All we could see were the outlines of houses and hedges. We walked across the field, all the way to the edge of the air base and then back, holding hands, sometimes talking, sometimes just walking.

★   ★   ★

After Schweinfurt the Eighth Air Force was put on stand-down for lack of enough operational aircraft to mount a major mission. We were waiting for replacements—both planes and crews—from the United States.

During the lull Margot and I made a short trip to Cambridge. Her in-laws in Norwich took her children for a couple of days, and off we went. It was the first time I'd traveled with an English-woman. This visit gave me another—and far better—perspective on Cambridge, where earlier I had been beaten and almost killed. Going there with Margot was entirely different and very civilized. We stayed at a small bed-and-breakfast which she knew. We had tea at a charming old guest house, and then we walked the grounds of the university. We strolled along the green, grassy banks of a placid, winding, narrow stream that was quite a contrast to the larger rivers back home. Willow trees dipped their branches into the water, and graceful swans went gliding by.

It was wonderful to be with Margot. I could talk to her, I liked her, and we had lovely sex. We often talked about her hus-band. She believed he was dead. She thought that if he had been captured, she would have heard by now that he was a prisoner of war. She missed him terribly. She was very much in love with him, and she had his children. She told me what he was like. His family had an accounting business in Norwich which he had been plan-ning to join. But the war came along first.

We spent two days and one night in Cambridge. It was a rare treat for us. Back at Snetterton Heath, Margot and I almost never went out. Her husband was well remembered, and she didn't want to provoke gossip that she was dating an American soldier, even though—or maybe because—it was happening all over Britain. I understood how she felt.

We took the train back to Snetterton Heath. I walked Margot to her cottage and returned to base to see what was happening. We were still on stand-down, but I noticed some new faces. Most of the new crews went into the 338th Squadron, which had suffered the most losses on the Schweinfurt raid.

*   *   *

Around this time I was awarded a Distinguished Flying Cross. Normally, the D.F.C. was given to fliers who had completed their full twenty-five missions. By October 1943 a few in our group had done that. I got my medal after my fifteenth mission because I had a couple of German fighters to my credit.

The heavy losses suffered in the Schweinfurt raid brought the strategy of daylight bombing back into question. The R.A.F. brass and Churchill himself had long wanted us to switch to night bombing. The question had been debated at the highest levels when Roosevelt and Churchill met at the Casablanca Conference back in January 1943. Eighth Air Force commander General Ira Eaker and other high brass went to Casablanca and made impassioned speeches about why they wanted to continue high-altitude daylight bombing.

If we had flown at night, it would have been more disastrous for us than for the English. One problem was that we were not trained in night flying, even though we often flew at night on the way home from missions. More significant, we found that a B-17's thirty-six flaming exhaust pipes could be seen a long way off at night. Finally, at night we would be a danger to each other. We had .50-caliber machine guns which could destroy a plane at a range of a thousand yards. The British had .30-calibers which had an effective range of just three to four hundred yards. Therefore, if we came under attack at night, we would be almost as likely to shoot down our own planes as enemy fighters.

We flew some practice missions at night, but we continued our daylight bombing. We also continued to have high casualties.

*   *   *

One evening I went to Margot's place. As usual, the door was unlocked. In the villages no one locked his door. Just as I started to push the door open, I heard voices. I looked in and saw an elderly couple sitting there, talking with Margot and playing with the children. I assumed they were her in-laws, so I closed the door quietly and tiptoed away. I didn't want to cause her any problems

125

by having them see an American G.I. visiting their son's widow and their grandchildren.

I decided to walk over to The Eccles Pub in another little village close to the base. In England the villages were sometimes just a mile or two apart. The Eccles Pub is still there today. When people go back to the base, they always visit the pub.

That was my first night at The Eccles. I walked in to find a typical smoky English pub with wood-paneled walls, hanging beer steins and wine glasses, and beer barrels with big brass taps. Spell, who was sitting with a lady friend, motioned me to come over. He was surprised to see me in the pub; he was a regular and had never seen me there. We had an enjoyable evening shooting the bull. Spell was given to a lot of good-natured teasing, and because I was the kid of the crew, I was often the butt of his jokes.

Then in came Johnny Hull, the gunner from New York whose father-in-law was a general. Johnny was the guy who had put the large bottle of Scotch on top of the door frame in our hut. He was a lot of fun, a good talker, always moaning and groaning about the fact that he was a sergeant and his father-in-law was a general who didn't want to or couldn't do anything for him. I think it was all said in a joking way.

This turned out to be a pleasant evening. All too soon it was closing time. Spell went somewhere with his girlfriend, and I walked back to the base with Johnny. His conversation turned serious. He told me his wife was a nice girl and he felt that her father, the general, was disappointed that she had married an enlisted man. But Johnny felt a lot of pride about being a flying sergeant in combat. We also talked about New York. He was a sophisticated guy, Johnny Hull, and how he ended up as a gunner I don't know. It seemed a lot more unlikely than my ending up as one.

This was one of the few times that I had one-on-one conversations with Hull and Spell. They were exceptional young men, really great guys. I think of all the people I had met in the Air Force up to that time, they were the best—the cream of the crop of young American men in this war.

Everything was dark in the hut, and we went to our respective bunks, undressed, and lay down. We were still on stand-down, so I didn't have to worry about a mission the next day. I had a luxurious sleep.

Chapter Ten

After the Schweinfurt mission it rained all the time—not just drizzle, but heavy rain. If you stepped off the boardwalks, you sank in mud up to your knees. It was the gooiest mess you could imagine. You couldn't use the bicycles except on the asphalt and the hard parts of the roads. You could never ride across a field on a bike.

Bicycles at the base were a funny thing. Nobody had his own; it wasn't necessary. Hundreds of bikes were stacked all around the huts, and they belonged to everybody, officers and enlisted men alike. When you needed one, you used it. A loose bike was yours to take wherever you wanted; when you came back, you left it in the general area. The only person who used a jeep was Colonel Old.

It's odd what you recall after all these years. For some reason I remember one guy who bet that if somebody brought him food, he could stay in bed for a week without getting out. He didn't even get up to go to the bathroom. I think he had some kind of a bedpan underneath his blankets. The stink got so bad that nobody could get within ten feet of him.

Everybody laid bets on him. Of course, it depended on the weather and other conditions. We were on stand-down, but if we were scheduled to fly, all bets were off. As it turned out, he stayed in bed for three days and nights before we flew. I would find that impossible. It's hard for me to go to sleep before 10:00 at night and to get up any later than 6:00 in the morning, even to this day.

I've been asked a few times what kind of toilet facilities the B-17 had. The answer is none.

Well, that's not quite right. There was a laughable attempt. Between the waist compartment and the tail, there was a tin can with a lid on it. You were supposed to sit down and defecate into that can. But on a mission, even if we managed to find the time to go—remember, that meant peeling off a number of layers of clothing—at high altitude, when you put your butt down on the toilet, the frozen metal would take part of your skin with it. So we just threw the damn thing out of the airplane.

Then, in the bomb bay, there was a pee tube—a funnel with a tube running out. You were supposed to make your way across this narrow catwalk with bombs hanging on both sides, unzip yourself in this extreme cold, aim into the funnel, and urinate. But if someone had already used it and if some of his urine had frozen and stopped up the tube, your pee splashed right back up in your face. So we abandoned the tube. If we had to go and if we had time, we unzipped and peed on the floor or out the waist window. I've seen urine freeze before it hit the waist window, then rattle around like tiny ice cubes. If we didn't have time to unzip, we just peed in our pants.

You had to watch what you ate and drank before flying. On long missions you might even regret a morning cup of coffee. I rarely ate before a mission, but I recall one time when I joined the crews who were having an early morning breakfast before briefing. Our flight surgeon, Doc Hartman, came in, looked at what we were being fed—eggs and beans—and stomped into the kitchen. We heard him angrily tell the mess sergeant he would force-feed him beans. Then he would make the sergeant fly to show him what happened when you ate beans and went up to high altitude.

Lieutenant Charles Blumenfeld, our navigator, always put on his oxygen mask when we were taking off. He'd put it on at the very beginning, even though most guys waited to put it on until we reached 10,000 feet. The problem was Lieutenant "Nocky" Johnson, who shared the front of the plane with Blumenfeld. Johnson, a big guy who ate a lot, had a nervous stomach and was exceedingly flatulent. Now, at altitude everybody farted; we couldn't help it. The higher we flew, the more the gases in our insides would expand. Way back in the waist of the B-17, we gunners had plenty of air flow to dissipate the great amount of gas we passed. But in the closed, cramped nose of the plane, the only protection Blumenfeld had was his oxygen mask. He complained bitterly that he would like Johnson off the crew because, he said, nobody farted so voluminously or with such a penetrating stench.

If you were desperate, there was only one place to take a crap: in your pants. It was an uncomfortable solution, to say the least. Unfortunately, our pilot and co-pilot, Tolbert and Macleod, were plagued by the need to evacuate, and they ended up defecating and urinating in their pants quite a bit. It was a common thing. Sometimes people had diarrhea. It was unpleasant, but we usually had no alternative. There was nothing to do but do it. As a result, there was no smell like the smell that greeted the ground crew when a combat crew came back from a particularly long and har-rowing mission. No one writes about this in the books that try to make war glamourous.

That brings to mind another unpleasant subject. Crabs were an epidemic in England at the time. Where they came from I don't know, but everyone had them. They were even on the toilets. We were given blue ointment that we'd put in our pubic hair or under the arms where they tended to congregate. I can think of nothing more horrible than the time I flew a mission with blue ointment in my armpits and my pubic area. My sweat and the heat from my electric suit drove those things deeper into my arm-pits. The itching was unbelievable. I nearly went crazy trying to scratch them through all the layers of my flying gear. I thought I was going to jump out of the airplane to get rid of the discomfort. Cobalt blue ointment, crabs, heat, sweat, and fear—that combina-tion is as close to hell as you can get, for my money.

★   ★   ★

Life went on at the air base. Planes were being patched up and engines were being rebuilt or repaired. Johnny Euhas came over to tell us he was going away to The Wash for a six-week gun-nery course. After the course he hoped to fly as a gunner on our crew. Since Bills had been killed, all of our engineer-gunners had been replacement gunners; in other words, we had different guys all the time. We would miss Johnny as crew chief because he was an efficient, knowledgeable engineer who had a good ground crew working with him. He was always concerned that our plane be at its best mechanically so it could bring us back.

A lot of my time was spent in idle conversations with the crews in our hut. All but two or three of these crews were new. Most of the other guys were gone—dead, missing, taken prisoner, wounded. No entire, original crew in our hut had yet finished a tour of duty.

Having completed about eighteen missions, I was considered a hardened veteran. I brooded quietly and waited for the next shoe to drop. Most of the time I tried not to think about what was going to happen.

On October 20, six days after the Schweinfurt mission, the Eighth Air Force was able to muster enough serviceable planes to mount a raid against Düren in northwestern Germany. Again, it was an early-morning briefing, a take-off into the cold, miserable, wet dawn, and a long flight to the target, where we ran into heavy flak and darting attacks by German fighters. Two of the 96th Bomb Group crashed in Holland on the way to Düren, but the *Black Hawk* made its pass and we dropped our bombs. I later learned there were few survivors of the two B-17s that went down in Holland. One fell on the Belgian-Dutch border. The other crashed into and demolished a farmhouse near Utrecht. Inside, a baby in a baby buggy was miraculously untouched.

It was incredibly cold that day. After we landed at home, we watched a bomber coming in and shooting off red flares, which indicated that there were wounded aboard. We could see a big gap in the front of the plane. We walked over to watch it as it taxied to the 338th's hardstand. The ambulance and fire truck came racing up. The medics pulled the bombardier out of the hole in the front of the plane. He had frozen to death.

At this point I was almost as afraid of the cold as I was of the flak and the fighters. You could die quickly from the cold. Sometimes the air temperature was sixty or seventy degrees below zero Fahrenheit, with 150-mile-an-hour winds blowing through the open waist windows and the radio hatch. During high-altitude missions that lasted long hours, our primitive electric suits and all the heavy clothing we could put on just barely kept us from freezing to death. The cold hurt; it penetrated with an intensity that was the same as pain. The cold was like a serpent crawling over my body, enveloping and numbing my mind, roaring into my ears, "Let me in. Let me in and I'll kill you."

When we fired our guns for a long time during a concentrated enemy fighter attack, the barrels would glow red hot even in the sub-zero temperatures of high altitude. It was alarming. We could sight down the barrels and see they had become warped and therefore inaccurate. So while the aircraft was bouncing around, often taking evasive action, we had to change barrels in a hurry. Sometimes the heat expanded the barrel so much that it wouldn't come off, and we had to use a .50-caliber bullet as a tool to loosen the barrel. We actually pounded on the barrel with a live round! I wonder how we did this without exploding the round—we were so violent and in such a hurry. Our hands were encumbered by all the layers of gloves we wore. I usually had to strip down to the bottom layer, my silk gloves, to get a better grip. My hand would nearly freeze during this short time.

One day all of our guns froze up at the breach despite the fact that we used special anti-freeze lubricants. Blumenfeld, our navigator, told us on the intercom that the outside temperature reading was seventy-two degrees below zero. The moving mechanism of my gun was locked with thin ice. I tried to thaw it with my gloves, to no avail. In horror I looked out of the waist window to see a squadron of ME-109s preparing to attack us. We decided to bluff—to move the guns around as if we were firing or preparing to fire. What a helpless feeling! Yet at the same time, I was relieved that this was one occasion when I would not have to kill anyone.

We moved our barrels menacingly and prayed. At the last second, the ME-109s climbed high above us, then dived, but they went after a lower formation. I wondered what would happen to the B-17s below us. But because they were a few hundred feet below us, the air was warmer and their machine guns were okay. They fought off the attack, and we were spared. Soon we dropped a few hundred feet and our guns warmed just enough to function. We were back in the killing business again.

When we came under flak attack, I would sometimes look at the ground below and see the flash of yellow lights from the anti-aircraft guns. I thought that I might see the flash of the 88-mm gun that would kill me. I would count to twelve. If I reached twelve and was still alive, the shell had either missed or exploded at the wrong altitude.

When the German fighter planes attacked, I could see their 20-mm cannon blinking at us, and I wondered how in the world they were missing. They always seemed to be aimed right at us. I realize now that I forgot to allow for how difficult a shot it was, since both planes were moving. And we were shooting back at them, which no doubt upset their pilots' aim a bit. Attacking a formation of B-17s bristling with .50-caliber guns must have been scary for the German fighter pilots. But they did their damnedest to shoot us down, and we did our damnedest to get them before they did.

November was a grim month. There were none of the losses on the scale of what we had suffered in October, but there were losses nevertheless. There were many other ways to die than being shot down or blown up by flak or fighters. Some were strange indeed. Planes collided with each other because of the bad weather and lack of visibility. Once, an aircraft came back from a mission with its entire oxygen system out. Two gunners were dead and a third was nearly dead because of cold and lack of oxygen. The third gunner wasn't wounded, but he was near death because his oxygen mask had frozen. His eyes were sealed by ice. Another gunner had to scrape his crewmate's eyelashes to free his eyelids.

To finish off a bad month, when we came back from a mission Thanksgiving Day, we were supposed to join a celebration with some U.S.O. group in the mess hall, but when we arrived there was nothing left to eat for the combat crews. It really pissed us off.

★   ★   ★

Before one briefing we had a lecture about something called heavy water that the Germans were working on. The heavy water could be used to produce a new type of explosive much more powerful than anything that was known to man. I didn't know at that time that they were talking about the development of a German atomic bomb.

The heavy water was being produced at Rjukan Dam in Norway. The Norwegian underground and the British command had been trying to take out the dam without success. We were scheduled to fly to Norway on November 16. Some bombers would be diverted to Bergen and some would bomb the Rjukan Dam. The flight would take almost eleven hours. We were given only half a load of bombs. In the other part of the bomb bay they put in "Tokyo tanks," long-distance tanks, so we would have enough gas. We were told to conserve fuel.

Everyone was dead tired from previous missions, and as we were leaving the briefing room, we noticed the flight surgeon, Doc Hartman, standing by a bowl of big red pills. He said that anybody who was tired and couldn't keep awake should take some. I took a handful and swallowed them. So did most everybody. Later on, I found out that they were amphetamines and that I had taken too many. In about an hour I was so wired that I could have flown without the airplane.

Off we went to Norway, flying near the Arctic Circle over some of the most beautiful countryside I have ever seen. My sightseeing was interrupted as we flew into a narrow valley and over the Rjukan Dam to drop our bombs. The bombs skidded off and had no effect whatsoever on the concrete dam. I don't think the pumphouse at the bottom was hit, either. Fortunately, there was no anti-aircraft fire.

Back at the base, when I tried to go to sleep, my bed seemed to be flying. I could not stop it. I felt like I was going to explode out of my skin. I never took those pills again.

★   ★   ★

Our new long-range fighter escorts, P-51 Mustangs, were going into action. But we had difficulty rendezvousing with them; sometimes they just weren't there, and I don't know why. On a few missions they jumped in unexpectedly and saved our necks, but I rarely saw P-51s actually flying in escort position.

I recall a mission in early December that gave us a scare. After our bombing run we came around in a half-circle and suddenly found ourselves practically at a standstill. B-17s were capable of a maximum airspeed in level flight of 160 to 165 miles per hour. Our engines were straining against high-altitude 150-mile-per-hour headwinds, and when I looked at the ground below, we were hardly moving forward at all. We were trapped in the sky like bugs in amber. We would have been almost stationary targets for German fighters. Fortunately, none appeared. Our group leader changed course to fly at an angle of thirty degrees to the wind, and we started to make a little headway. Then we descended to lower altitudes and finally found lesser headwinds. The trip back home was much longer, but we were happy just to make it.

The Cold Blue Sky

On December 13 we were briefed for a mission to Kiel. For this attack the 96th Bomb Group put up a record fifty-four aircraft. As in the Schweinfurt raid, we had to form an A group and a B group. But *Black Hawk* had to abort before reaching the target because of mechanical problems. We made it home and landed safely, with no feelings of guilt. There was no way we could have continued. Of course, it didn't count as a mission for us.

We got back at about 1100 hours, dog tired. We returned to the hut and went to sleep. At about 1500 hours—3:00 p.m.—we heard the planes returning. Then we heard a tremendous explosion. I got up and ran down toward the field. Lieutenant Fabian's plane, the *Dottie J II,* had crashed. His crew's enlisted men shared our hut. I was told that Fabian's B-17 had mechanical problems and had been signaling that they had to land immediately, but unfortunately another plane had flown in front of them. They had to pull up abruptly and couldn't make it back around, so they crash-landed into a nearby field.

Of Fabian's crew of ten, six survived and four were killed. The dead included the navigator, Lieutenant John Boyd; Truman Starr, a dark-haired fellow whom I liked a lot; and James Mabry, the guy who took me on the motorcycle ride to London. The other fatality was an officer whom I didn't know. Joe Tonko, whom I've already mentioned, and Jay Epright, the guy who always said he would never make it home, were injured.

After the ambulances pulled away, Tex Shields and I, along with a couple of others from our hut, walked down to the hospital to visit the injured men. Then we decided to go to the morgue to look at the remains of our friends. When we got there, one of the enlisted medical staff who knew us came up and said, "Please don't go in there." I looked in the door, and the medics were going through a pile of body parts trying to pick out pieces of identification from escape kits. It looked like a mess of garbage. It was a horror. We quickly turned around and walked toward the hospital. When we got there, the doctor wouldn't let us see the survivors. They were sedated and pretty much beaten up, but lucky. If you saw pictures of those wrecked planes, you'd wonder how anyone survived such terrible crashes.

Back at the hut, I found it difficult to look at the empty beds. I felt nothing, or at best, I felt glad it wasn't me. I thought of myself as uncaring and uninterested. It hadn't paid to make friends with the three enlisted men on Fabian's crew who shared our hut. Now, looking back, I think I was protecting myself—otherwise, I couldn't have continued to fly those missions day after day. I was committed to finishing my tour of duty for my own sense of self-worth. I was from an ordinary background, uneducated, and used to hard work. I avoided fights by not being too "macho" (although none of us knew that term back then). Maybe I needed to be a soldier for my ego. Maybe I needed it to feel like a man. At the time, all I knew was that I had to do it.

I can't explain why we bomber crews, without any gung-ho attitude at all, would put our lives on the line mission after mission against the terrible odds of those days. I do not understand my blind obedience. I don't regret it, but I can't explain it. Even when my fears were about to overwhelm me, even when I was physically sick, I kept flying my missions. I didn't want to let my crewmates down. I would rather have been dead.

Right after Fabian's crash, Tex Shields came up to me and asked if I wanted to go with him to take Mabry's body to the American Air Force cemetery in London. I declined. I didn't want to ride all that way in an ambulance with the body. I just couldn't do it. So Tex went by himself, and as it turned out, that decision saved his life. And who knows? Perhaps my decision not to go with Tex but to fly the next mission saved my own crew's lives. A second's lag in a gunner's reaction could mean the difference between survival and destruction for aircraft and crew. They were a lot better off with me than with some replacement gunner.

On December 16 we were scheduled for another raid on Bremen. This was another target whose very name inspired fear because it was so heavily defended by anti-aircraft guns and the many German fighter bases surrounding the city. In the past we had penetrated Bremen through black clouds of flak and explosions. But on our approach into Bremen that day we ran into very light flak and no enemy fighters. It was most unusual. We were supposed to have P-51 Mustangs escorting us, but when we looked around, we couldn't see them. On the other hand, that may be why there were no German fighters.

As we flew into and then out of the target area, I had a feeling almost of peace and contentment. We—the 337th—were the leading squadron, and our *Black Hawk* led the squadron. We were well on our way home when I saw a group of fighters too far away for me to recognize. I picked up the binoculars which we carried in the waist and tried to identify them, but the plane was shaking too much and I couldn't focus. I called the pilot and said there were about sixty or seventy fighters about a mile and a half away. I couldn't identify them. Tolbert replied that there were P-51s in the area but said to keep our eyes open.

We made a wide turn and headed out over the Zuider Zee. Thick clouds rose high above us. All of a sudden, I saw fighters with swastikas closing on us in a steep dive at over 400 miles per hour. We were struggling along at about 165. That made for a closing speed of close to 600 miles per hour. They went by so fast I couldn't aim my gun. I didn't get off a single shot.

Explosions followed, and planes in our squadron started going down. Looking behind and above us, I saw Schroeder's plane explode. I saw Clarence Kelley's ball turret fall away free from what had been the belly of the plane. We flew on, and as I looked around, I realized we were the only plane leading the formation. Out of seven planes in our squadron, six were gone. It was as if a giant hand had swept the sky clean of everyone but us.

We flew on, expecting to be wiped out at any moment, but the German fighters didn't return. Maybe they had just enough fuel left for that one terrible swing through the formation. We joined up with the rest of the group and flew on home. *Black Hawk*, the only survivor of the 337th Bomb Squadron, came back without a single hole.

Captain Tolbert parked our plane, and we took our gear and walked down the slight hill toward the buildings. I was all but in shock. The ground crews came out to take care of the aircraft and asked us where everybody was. It was almost dark. I turned around and looked back up the rising ground toward the *Black Hawk*. You could just see its solitary silhouette in the last light of day. I said, "They're all gone." They looked at us with incredulous eyes.

Then we went on to the briefing room and tried to tell what happened. Apparently somebody decided that Schroeder's plane had collided with another B-17 from our squadron; at least, that's what our unit history says. But that's not the way I remember it.

Our ball turret gunner Dutch Eisenhower, our tail gunner Vic Hunt, and I all thought the German fighters shot it down. In my mind's eye I can still see that plane blowing up and Clarence Kelley's ball turret falling away.

Hardly a week goes by when I don't stop to think about Kelley and Johnny Hull and their crewmates. I had known them so well, but for such a short time. I hope they went quickly without pain or suffering.

Driving from Chicago to Florida in 1947, I made a short detour to Bainbridge, Georgia, where Kelley had grown up. I had no address for him, so I went to the local police station and talked to the police chief, who looked like Rod Steiger, pot belly and all. The chief knew the family; he knew everybody in town. He called the Kellys and offered to take me to their home. On the way there in his squad car, he asked me what my business was with the Kellys. He knew that the son Clarence had been lost in the war and was still listed as missing in action. I told him I had served with Kelley and had seen him go down.

We drove to the house and parked. Cars were pulling up. Kelley's mother, sisters, and other relatives were sitting on the porch. I went up and told Mrs. Kelley who I was and how I had been so fond of her son. And that I had flown alongside him on his last day and that there were no survivors. She brought out photo albums of Clarence. We all talked about him, and we all cried. Then Mrs. Kelley went inside and came back with a letter. It was from Clarence. I read it. It said, "Mother, I know I will not survive this terrible war. But you are not to worry because I have made my peace with Jesus."

That Bremen mission was the first for Johnny Euhas, our former maintenance crew chief, newly trained and flying with us as a replacement engineer and top turret gunner. (A master sergeant, he was the highest-ranking gunner in the entire Bomb Group.) I remember falling asleep on the way to the target and being awakened by Johnny's shrill voice on the intercom. He was nervous and wanted to know if anything was happening.

What a first mission it turned out to be! After we landed, Johnny got out through the front end of the plane and came walking back as Jimmy Spell, the other gunners, and I were getting out of the rear hatch. Johnny asked Spell, "Jimmy, what kind of a mission was this today?" Jimmy looked him straight in the eye and said, "A fucking milk run."

On that mission some of our planes fell into the Zuider Zee, and others crashed among Dutch villages. We later learned that Dutch civilians found the wreckage and gathered up many of the bodies. Personnel from a nearby Luftwaffe air base took the dead and gave them a military burial.

In most of the actions I had seen, at least some of the crews were able to bail out when their planes were hit. But on the Bremen mission, almost nobody got out. An exception was one of our group's great planes, *Fertile Myrtle*, which had flown lead on the Regensburg shuttle and the Schweinfurt mission. *Myrtle* struggled home wounded and crashed in England; the crew bailed out.

After debriefing, I went back to the hut—once again, an empty hut. Out of eighteen men who had slept there the previous night, only the five of us from *Black Hawk* were left. I couldn't go in. I wasn't hungry, but I went to the mess hall thinking some of our crew would be there. I found Johnny Euhas, who wanted to talk about his first mission. I just wanted to sit with a living being. After my favorite meal of canned pears, English bread, and coffee, I went back to the hut. I was afraid as I opened the door. Beds were unmade, photos were on the shelf, and personal items reminded me that their owners were gone, dead. It was spooky.

Tex Shields, a member of Fabian's crew, had not yet come back from accompanying Mabry's body to London. What a lousy surprise was waiting for him. Later that evening, I heard somebody coming up the wooden walkway, and in came Tex. He asked, "Where's everybody?"

I looked at him and said, "They're gone."

He said, "What do you mean, they're gone?"

"Either they were blown up, or there was a collision, and we're all that's left. We lost six planes of the squadron."

"They bail out?"

"No, nobody bailed out."

He started to cry. He was their lucky charm, he said, and if he had been there, it wouldn't have happened. We tried to reassure him that it would have happened and he could not have prevented it. He would have been as dead as anybody and he should be happy he was alive. But he didn't hear any of that. He just cried and cried.

To this day I can see Tex sitting on his bunk crying, then going through the personal effects of his friends to sort out what he could before the graves registration people came in and took all the clothes away. That's what we always did—we salvaged what we could use, mostly items of clothing, to replace our things that were worn out. Of course we didn't take any personal effects; those were sent to the families. Tex wandered around like a robot looking for things that he could send home to their families.

They were gone, the enlisted men I knew: Irvin Wade, Art Demieux, Clarence Kelley, Carpentieri the waist gunner, and my good friend from New York, Johnny Hull. I looked up at the top of the door frame. Johnny's bottle of Red Label Scotch was still there, waiting for New Year's Eve. But he wouldn't be there to drink it.

Not only was our own hut empty, but the crews in the huts around us had also been practically wiped out. Almost the only ones left were the few replacement crews who didn't fly that day. Because of all the deaths and injuries, we were short of trained crews, and we had to wait for new crews to arrive. It was shortly before Christmas 1943. I started imagining the scenes back home as the families got the news that their sons and husbands were dead or horribly wounded. The more I thought about it, the bleaker I felt. What a Christmas for them!

I managed to write a page to my family every day to let them know I was still alive, but sometimes they didn't get the mail for two or three weeks. Then they would get a bunch of letters all at once. I found out later that our raids were making headlines back home, where the newspapers would report twenty-eight bombers missing, fifty bombers missing, sixty bombers missing. I can imagine how terrified my family was. I also thought about how difficult it must be for my older brother, stationed in Washington state, knowing of the woes of the family and how frightened they were. I'm sure it wasn't much fun for him when he came home on furlough and tried to cheer them up.

A few days went by, but I could still hardly bear to go into our nearly empty barracks. With Vic Hunt in the hospital and Hubner and Bills gone, only Dutch Eisenhower, Jimmy Spell, Tex Shields and I were left in the hut. God, what a bleak time that was.

I went down to see Hunt at the big evacuation hospital and found him sitting in a wheelchair, flirting with all the nurses. His girlfriend was a nurse who was a lieutenant. That was unusual. Enlisted men and female officers just did not mix in the Army at that time.

Jay Epright came back from the hospital. He hadn't been wounded too badly when Fabian's B-17 crashed. I remember saying to him, "Well, your worst is over, you survived the crash." He said, "That's not it, there's still more to come for me." That sent cold chills up my spine.

Bremen was my twenty-fourth mission. I had one more to fly before I could go home. I had more than tripled the seven-mission average life expectancy of our crews. I was two or three missions ahead of the rest of the *Black Hawk* crew because of the extra missions I had flown with other crews early on. If I finished my tour of duty I'd be the second on the crew to go home. For our navigator Lieutenant Charles Blumenfeld, who had also flown some extra missions, Bremen was the twenty-fifth.

I became frozen in time. I turned into a robot just waiting for my last mission. I woke up, I went to the bathroom, I tried to keep myself clean. I'd eat occasionally. But the whole time I talked to no one. The weather was constantly cold and rainy. I imagine the weather over Europe was just as bad, so we were on hold while I waited and waited for what would surely be my last mission one way or the other. I couldn't even bring myself to visit Margot, although I did go to the pub with her one evening.

The area soon started to fill up again with new crews. No one new had come into our hut yet, for which I was grateful. Their fresh, enthusiastic faces turned glum when they learned whom they were replacing and what had happened to their predecessors. They were scared before they started—and with good reason.

At that point, amidst all the loss and grief, I saw myself as a hard, cold, uncaring human being. I didn't understand the psychology of my defenses: that by being cold and uncaring and shutting myself off from all the pent-up emotion, I was able to stay sane. But, primitive as it was, it worked. Practically the only emotion I had left was fear.

I kept wondering what kind of last mission I would draw. Maybe I would be lucky and just have to cross the Channel on a milk run, maybe to bomb some airfield in France. I hoped it wouldn't be Bremen again, or anywhere in Germany. I didn't know if I could face that.

On December 23 I went down to the mail room. The mail clerk, using a big hand stamp, was stamping "DECEASED" on a stack of envelopes. I looked at what he was doing and saw that they were letters from home for Clarence Kelley. I wondered how long it took for his friends and family to find out he was dead.

The survivors of Fabian's crew got out of the hospital. A crew was put together based on the remnants of Fabian's crew, with Fabian as pilot. Johnny Euhas became that crew's engineer and top turret gunner, and Tex Shields was assigned as the radio man. It was good for Tex to fly with Fabian's crew because he knew these guys well. Fabian's and Schroeder's crews had trained together. They would be flying the next mission alongside our plane.

On Christmas Eve we had to get away from the base, so I walked over to The Eccles Pub with Spell and Tex Shields. For the first time in my life, I got drunk. On port wine. Was I sick afterward! We staggered back to our hut. Nothing was happening on the base, no putt-putt of engines or anything like that, so there was no mission scheduled for Christmas Day. We slept in Christmas morning. Later, the mess hall tried to get together some sort of a Christmas dinner—turkey, cranberries, sweet potatoes, and mashed potatoes. I managed to eat a little bit. The day crept slowly by. Then the night crept by. The next day crept by. And the next, and the next. Finally, on December 30 we were alerted for a mission on the last day of the year.

I didn't sleep much that night. I heard the Charge of Quarter's footsteps and was wide awake before he opened our door. As we got dressed, nobody mentioned that it was my last mission. Then at briefing, I looked at the map, and damn! The red ribbon went deep into Germany's heavily-defended industrial heartland, the Ruhr Valley. Target: the city of Ludwigshaven. No milk run for me. We were supposed to have fighter escort, but based on previous experience, I wasn't counting on it.

After the briefing we went to get our equipment and rode a truck out to the plane. As I was climbing into the airplane, Captain Tolbert came over to me and said, "Sergeant, I wish we had an easier one for your last one today, but don't you worry, I'll get you back home safely." I shook his hand and got in the airplane. Dominic and I got our waist positions ready. We secured our guns, put our ammo into the feeders, hooked up our ammunition and stowed it, made sure the safety was on, and waited for take-off. I was both hoping the mission would be scrubbed and hoping it wouldn't be. I wanted to get it over with so I could know I was alive and had survived and go home. Yet I also wanted to postpone this final reckoning.

Green flares shot up, and we followed other planes in our group onto the runway. As we roared into the air, I said to myself, "Well, that's one last take-off." I got into position and then started silently counting off the minutes: "That's one minute less I have to worry about... That's another minute less I have to worry about." I kept that up and started praying that I would get home safely. I listened to the engines to see if there was any kind of defect because now that we'd started out, I sure didn't want to abort and have to sweat out another take-off and another landing. To my relief, the engines were running well.

A little later in the flight, I felt ice trickling down my spine. It was a weird sensation. At first I thought some sweat on my back had frozen. But no, that wasn't so. It was just that my spine felt like ice was dripping down it. I'd never had that sensation before. It must have been the fear. I took slow, steady breaths to counter the panic, if that's what it was. I didn't actually feel panicky, I just felt encased in ice, with my back being the coldest part.

I leaned out the waist window and watched and waited for a fighter attack. But on and on we flew, and no fighters appeared. Finally, I saw a flight of P-51s swoop by and take their position with the leading planes up ahead. By this time, we were above 10,000 feet and had finished our oxygen check. Later we reached 31,000 feet, which was unusually high. Very rarely did we climb beyond 27,000 feet. I guess we went that high to avoid clouds and turbulence at lower altitudes.

The seconds dragged by like hours. At last we approached Ludwigshaven. I could see the flak bursting around the aircraft of the First Division. We made a 180-degree turn toward the initial point where we would start our bomb run. And then we were swallowed up by intense flak bursting all around us, shaking and rocking us all over the sky. Johnson, the bombardier, signaled that he had the plane under control, and Tolbert released his controls. Johnson flew the plane until we dropped our bombs. So far, despite a thick carpet of flak, nothing had happened to us.

When we were on the way out of the target area, I said to myself, "Well, that's done with so far." Then I began to wonder about fighter opposition. The only fighters I had seen so far were our P-51s. I was wondering where the German fighters were and wondering where our P-51s were. Again, I counted the seconds.

Finally, as we approached the coast at an altitude of about 10,000 feet, I could smell the sea. I could always smell the sea, just as I could smell land coming back to England. And I thought, "My God, now if nothing happens, if there are no mechanical problems, no mid-air collisions, if there's no last-minute fighter attack, if we land safely, I'll be home. I'll be home free." I held my breath and waited. Finally, there was England. I could smell land, and I could see the white cliffs of Dover up ahead. I took out my celebratory Milky Way bar, frozen hard as a rock, and started chewing on it.

Over the air base we circled in perfect formation. Our group hadn't had a single loss that day. I was very, very thankful. I knew personally of guys—of entire crews—who were shot down or killed on their last missions. Of course, there were also guys who got it on their first missions.

We landed, and Tolbert came back to me and said, "See, I told you I'd get you home." Dutch Eisenhower came over and hugged me. Spell slapped me on the back, and Dominic came over and kissed me on the cheek. I appreciated those guys. They still had a few more missions to go.

I went to debriefing, then over to the 337th orderly room to speak to the operations officer. "Sir," I said, "Would you just check and make sure that today was my last mission, because I sure don't want to make any mistakes." And he looked at me and he said, "Yes, it's your last mission, Sergeant, but I don't want you to forget that you're still in the Army."

When I heard that, my life was transformed. I was alive. I had just been reborn, this time as an adult. In all my life, I have never experienced such a feeling of pure joy. I looked around, and everything took on a new meaning. The trees, the grass, the crops in the fields—everything was bathed in a new light. The colors were vivid. Mundane, everyday sights became interesting and significant. Everything troubling fell away.

I was like a snake shedding his old skin. I had such a delight in being alive and being able to see and smell and hear that I couldn't contain myself. I ran out into the field and just ran and ran and ran until I dropped. Then I came back to the barracks. I didn't know how to act. I wanted to be quiet. I didn't want to upset the guys who still had to fly their missions; they were probably dealing with the same kinds of fears that I had felt. But I was still exhilarated.

I thought that I should go see Margot and tell her the good news. But then I thought that I didn't want to do that, because it would be like saying goodbye. I would be leaving, and she would be staying. I don't think there was any way she was going to leave England with her two children. Then again, maybe she would have. Maybe she wanted to. Maybe that was the reason she liked me so much. But I had no intention of going home with a bride.

It was New Year's Eve. Jimmy Spell, Dutch Eisenhower, Hunt, Epright, and I were alone in the barracks. No new replacement crews had come in yet. We looked up at Johnny Hull's bottle of Scotch and decided that we were going to drink it all down and toast New Year's Eve and Johnny's memory.

So Jimmy climbed up and got the Scotch off the door frame and uncorked it. Since we had no glasses, we were going to swig it out of the bottle. He took a big swig of the bottle and grimaced in horror. Then he spit it out. I said, "What's wrong, Jimmy?" He said, "Johnny Hull fucked us. This isn't Scotch, it's just colored water." It was macabre—almost like Hull reaching out from the grave to smack us in the faces, however lovingly. The joke was on us. We spent the evening reminiscing.

I have never forgotten that evening. It spoiled New Year's Eves for the rest of my life. Nor have I forgotten that sad Christmastime of 1943. The guys from Schroeder's and Fabian's crew remain in my memory, never to grow old.

Chapter Eleven

After my last mission I wasn't sure what my duties were going to be or when I was going to go home. We were never told in advance what our futures would be once we had finished the required number of missions. Because of the low survival rate, experienced gunners were rare, so the Army Air Force decided to make us instructors in the gunnery schools in England.

I was called into group headquarters the next day. Colonel Travis told me I was going to stay on with the 96th Bomb Group as a gunnery instructor. A lot of new crews were arriving, and they wanted an experienced gunner for indoctrination.

Then he said, "I have another alternative that you might be interested in. We're creating what we call group gunnery officers, and they're going to fly one out of every three missions. Their job is to stay in the radio room and coordinate group gunnery procedures. We would be offering a direct field commission to first lieutenant. Would you be interested in anything like that? You'd have to volunteer for another tour of duty."

I thought about it for a minute. The idea of becoming a first lieutenant was tempting, but at the moment I felt that I had enough. I said no. So I became a gunnery instructor for the 96th—for how long, I didn't know.

A new crew—I think it was Richard Stakes' crew—was assigned to our hut and to me for indoctrination in whatever lessons I had learned in combat. We had set up a little classroom on the base where I took the enlisted men to talk about gunnery procedure. But all they wanted to know was how are the local girls, and how is London, and how often do we get passes. They let me know that they had been pretty well trained back in the United States. I listened without making a direct reply, and I kept on hammering away at gunnery procedure. I showed some combat films and tried to talk about aiming and firing, ammo and tracers, German fighter tactics, and things of that sort.

It wasn't hard to make myself heard. I was fairly well respected because there were hardly any guys around who had finished their tour of duty. I was a living example of an airman who had survived.

I spent about two weeks with these guys. We finally went up in the B-17 that they were going to fly on missions. We flew out over The Wash for some gunnery practice. There were targets in the area, and we would swoop down and they would learn to use their machine guns. I was to correct their aim and teach them accurate firing procedures. We flew down to The Wash maybe two or three times for target practice, then I accompanied them on practice missions.

Finally, they were alerted for a real mission. As usual, the crews were awakened at 0300 hours. I decided to go to briefing with them and help out as much as I could. I would find out where they were going, talk to them about the target if I knew anything about it, give them a hand loading up, and watch them take off.

So I went to breakfast with them, then went down to briefing and saw where the target was. "My God, this is a milk run," I told the guys, and they looked happy. I said, "This is good for you guys. You'll make a combat flight and get credit for a mission, and it's easy. You just cross the Channel to bomb." I think they were going to the Pas de Calais—not to the submarine pens which we had raided, but to the sites where the Germans were erecting rocket launchers. The target was right on the Channel coast, so it was just a matter of hitting land, coming across the target, coming back out to sea and coming back home. They would have fighter escort all the way in and back.

We finished breakfast. The crew picked up their guns, and we went to the plane. I stood there talking to the waist gunners. There was one waist gunner in particular whose hand I shook. I don't remember his name. I said to him, "You know, this is really good for you, going on a milk run," and he smiled. He seemed to be relieved. I noticed he was still nervous, with the gun kind of jiggling in his hand, and I remembered how I felt on my first mission. I went up to him and helped steady him, and we inserted the gun barrel together and screwed it into the machine gun mounting. He smiled again. I waited for him until they got the green flares and waved him off, watched him and waved to him until they were out of sight.

Then I waited for them to come back. Well, they didn't come back. They were the only plane lost by the 96th Bomb Group that day. They got hit by flak and, according to witnesses, they all bailed out. Later, I found out that five of the crew had been killed while bailing out. So much for milk runs.

I went back to the hut completely dead inside. I said to myself, "That's the last time I'm going to wish anybody good luck and say that they're going on a milk run." I felt like I had jinxed them.

Then I looked over at one of the crew's bed and saw a beautiful new flight jacket. Mine was grungy and torn up and spotted with oil. So I decided that I would, as spoils of war, take his flight jacket. It fit me well. About six weeks later, I was in the hut, and the door opened and in came this absolutely bald guy. He came up to me and said, "Milk run, you son of a bitch!" I thought he was going to deck me. And then he looked at me and said, "You have my jacket on!" and started laughing. I still have the flight jacket to this day.

This was the waist gunner whom I had helped out. He had bailed out of the aircraft, had been picked up by the French Underground, and had been escorted over the Pyrenees into Spain by a guide in the dead of winter. On the other side he was arrested by Spanish soldiers and thrown into jail along with a couple of other crew members who had evaded the Germans. The jailers shaved his head. He had been locked up for almost six weeks when he was found by an American consular official who constantly toured Spanish jails and villages looking for escaped American airmen. Before he knew it, his crewmates and he had been cleaned up, put on a plane in Lisbon, and sent back to England.

From England he was going to be sent back to the U.S. for reassignment, probably to the Pacific. Once you were shot down and escaped, you did not fly in the same combat theater. The brass was afraid that if the Germans shot you down again, you might be treated as a spy because you would have reported everything that you saw on the ground the first time.

Fifty years later, I attended a reunion of the 96th Bomb Group and the 337th Bomb Squadron at Dyess Air Force Base near the West Texas town of Abilene. We sat down to dinner, and the master of ceremonies called the names of guys and certain groups to stand up. For example, he asked, "Who was a prisoner of war?" and "Who was successful in evading after bailing out from a plane?"

When he asked that last question, a man at my table stood up. I looked at him and said, "When were you shot down?" And he answered, "I think it was January the fifth or something like that."

I said, "Was it on a mission across the Channel to Pas de Calais?"

"Yeah," he said.

"What is your name, sir?" I asked.

And he said, "Lieutenant Graverholtz." He was the navigator of that same crew. I told him the story of what had happened. I was glad to see another survivor from that crew. We talked, and I learned that he has a ranch in Texas.

I continued with my gunnery instruction. New crews were coming in all the time. I hope I was helpful in keeping some of those guys alive. I no longer wished anybody good luck, but I still walked them to their planes and helped them get ready. Then I saluted them as they took off.

Meanwhile, the rest of my crew—Tolbert's crew—had safely finished their twenty-five missions. Before his last mission our bombardier, "Nocky" Johnson, became so nervous that Doc Hartman ended up going with him on the flight. I know that these members of our crew finished their twenty-five missions: Captain James Tolbert, Lieutenants Norman Macleod, Charles Blumenfeld, and "Nocky" Johnson, and Sergeants Dutch Eisenhower, James Spell, and myself. Sergeant Victor Hunt was still in the hospital recovering from his wounds and never returned to active duty. I left England before Sergeant Dominic Beneditto finished his tour, and I never learned what happened to him.

I was maintaining a fairly busy training schedule and beginning to feel like an old relic at nineteen. I was seriously reconsidering the offer of a field commission to fly one out of every three missions. In the evenings I'd see Margot and sometimes stay all night with her. But a distance was starting to open between us. I guess it was a self-protective reaction on both our parts.

I hadn't been to London for some time and decided to take an overnight leave there. There was no place to sleep. Every hotel, inn, and bed-and-breakfast in the city was booked. The streets were just as crowded. There were uniforms from all sorts of outfits I'd never seen before. The ground forces were getting ready for the invasion of France. Back at the base they had told us that we were going to see more ships out in the sea and that the bomber crews were going to fly many missions in preparation for the invasion.

There I was in London without a place to sleep. At about nine o'clock, tired and hungry, I was walking along when a well-dressed gentleman in his late fifties stopped me and asked, "Do you need some help, soldier?"

We started talking. During the war, he said, he had traveled to Chicago many times. We found out that we were both of Jewish descent. I told him that the places I usually stayed were full and that the town was exceptionally crowded. "Oh, I know of a place I think you can stay," he said. "It might not be the most comfortable place in the world, but some friends of mine can help." Then he added, "Maybe you'll have dinner with me there. Sometimes they also have some kosher things." "Jesus, I would love to have some gefilte fish," I said.

He led me to a place which turned out not to be a real hotel but a clean flophouse. The tiny little "Hotel" sign outside was illuminated by a dimly burning bulb and invisible from ten feet away. We walked up the stairs and were greeted by the two men who owned the hotel. They were sure they could get me a room. "But it'll be expensive," they said. They charged me thirty pounds—the equivalent of about $130 at the time.

We went down to the restaurant. The hour was late, and we were the only people eating there. They brought out some gefilte fish. They had a little horseradish which wasn't bad, but it was the worst gefilte fish I ever ate in my life. It was like eating sawdust with a little bread and a flavoring of fish. It was a grotesque meal, but since my new acquaintance had invited me, I managed to swallow some of it.

After dinner I thanked him and went over to find my room. When I opened the door, I couldn't believe it. The room was precisely the size and width and depth of the single bed. To get both into the room and the bed, I had to open the door and step on the bed. I shut the door, hung up my clothes, and started to go to sleep—only to be awakened almost immediately by the sound of lovemaking in the rooms on either side of me. Then it dawned on me that the reason my room was so expensive was that I had rented it for the whole night, while normally the rooms were rented to prostitutes for half an hour or even fifteen minutes at a time.

I finally fell asleep. Then, at about 2:00 in the morning, I was awakened by air raid sirens. Right next door was an anti-aircraft battery. I heard a few bomb explosions go off, but mostly I heard the racket of the anti-aircraft guns—in addition to the noise of my neighbors. When I left in the morning, the owner asked me how my night was. I looked at him and said, "I hope you're not serious." He smiled, and out I walked.

I walked to Liverpool Street station and caught a train. I got back to the base, checked in, and went to the hut where Tex and Fabian's new crew had stayed. They weren't there. The hut had been cleaned up, and the beds were neatly made. I went to operations to find out what happened. They were listed as missing in action. I was told that they were last seen leaving the formation with two smoking engines and that nobody had been seen bailing out.

Well, there it went again. These were my last friends other than my crewmates who had finished all their missions.

The next morning I went through the briefing procedure with one of crews I had been training. They were scheduled to fly in our old plane, the *Black Hawk*. I think the new pilot who took over the crew was Lieutenant Pond.

I decided to walk down and look at the *Black Hawk*. It had patches all over it, and there was still one big hole in the waist compartment. On the floor was a red puddle. I found out that both waist gunners had been badly wounded on the last mission, and here was this big puddle of blood and urine. I called the crew chief over and just blew my stack. I was yelling and asking why it hadn't been cleaned up and why they were going to let a crew fly in this piss and blood which was not only demoralizing, but would also freeze at altitude and be slippery. I was very angry. I knew that when Johnny Euhas was a crew chief, he would have never allowed this. They quickly cleaned it up.

One day soon afterwards I volunteered to fly a mission with the crew, thinking I was going to witness D-Day. We crossed the Channel at a relatively low altitude, 10,000 feet, and wherever I looked I saw hundreds of ships—battleships, cruisers, destroyers, merchant ships, landing craft. But to our disappointment, it was a practice D-Day, not the real thing.

On March 6, 1944 Eighth Air Force heavy bombers, escorted all the way by P-51 fighters, attacked Berlin. They suffered heavy losses to determined Luftwaffe opposition. Sixty-nine U.S. bombers—of the 500 or so sent against the target—and eleven fighters were shot down. The formation was twice as big as when we had been there, so the percentage losses were less than we had suffered, but for the guys to whom it happened and their families, it was terrible. The 96th Bomb Group, far back in the bomber stream, was untouched. But the next day the 96th took the lead in another big attack on Berlin and had six B-17s shot down (of the thirty it put in the air).

My thoughts turned to the possibility of going back home and getting a furlough to visit my family. In early March I was called to operations, where I was told that my papers had come and I was to report to the Embarkations Center in Liverpool. I said goodbye to Spell, Eisenhower, and the rest of my crew who were still there. I went to visit Margot for the last time. It was a sad, tearful goodbye. My heart felt heavy to leave her, but at the same time I felt somehow relieved.

I packed up what belongings I had and, without looking back, caught the train to Liverpool. I reported to the Embarkations Center, where I had to wait for the first transportation available. Sometimes there was a plane, but if not, we had to wait for an empty ship going back. The big ocean liners were carrying thousands and thousands of troops from the U.S. to England for the invasion.

Walking into the barracks area, I ran into two guys with whom I had flown in the 95th Bomb Group. They were both from Tyler, Texas, and they had flown together and survived together, successfully completing their twenty-five missions. It was nice to see them.

The Cold Blue Sky

Finally, we were driven by truck to the dock area in Liverpool to board the *U.S.S. George Washington*. It was an old ship, a pre-World War One luxury liner. When we came aboard, one of the ship's crew told me that it had originally been named the *Bremen* and had been taken by the United States government from the Germans for reparations after World War One. What a way to go back home—on a German ship called the *Bremen*. I was a little uneasy about it. The name of that city stirred bad memories.

There were 300 of us, all airmen, going back on the *Bremen* —I mean the *George Washington*. Half were walking wounded, and there were nurses and medical attendants aboard to take care of them. The rest of us were airmen who had finished our tours of combat duty. On the trip from the States to Europe, this ship carried about 4,000 troops, so we 300 weren't many.

We were sailing with a fast convoy under blackout conditions. There were still German submarines out there. Because we were going to zigzag across the northern Atlantic, the usual five- or six-day voyage was probably going to take about two weeks.

Once on board, we went to our assigned quarters and stowed our gear. Some of the guys had brought along stuff you wouldn't believe. I didn't bring any arms back; we weren't allowed to. But a lot of the guys had arms. One guy had a disassembled .50-caliber machine gun.

Then we went up on deck to await departure. A bunch of ambulances pulled up, along with some trucks carrying military police. About fifty M.P.s jumped out of the trucks and formed double lines leading to the gangway. Then out of the ambulances came pairs of M.P.s with a guy in handcuffs and leg shackles between them. There were about thirty of these prisoners. I said, "My God, they're coming aboard with us!" Up the gangway they marched. I said, "Jesus, I'm glad they're coming with these M.P.s. These guys look like desperadoes."

But after about half an hour, all the M.P.s left. I said, "They're going to leave those guys on board with us without M.P.s?" Well, about three minutes later, our names started being called. We were told to appear in the captain's quarters. We dutifully marched there, to find a major who was the ranking military officer on board. He said, "Did you see those men come aboard?" I told him we had. Then he said, "Well, these are desper-

152

ate men. Half of them are in for murder. They're all going back to Leavenworth, life sentences, some under the possibility of death. The minimum sentence of any of the prisoners is thirty years. Armed robbery, rape, you name it—this is what they're accused of—and gentlemen, you are going to be responsible for them for the rest of the voyage."

I couldn't believe it! What were we going to guard them with? The major continued, "I'm sure you guys can raise some weaponry amongst yourselves." Then he ended with, "You're going to be on four-hour stints. Divide it among yourselves."

We walked down to the brig, which was all the way at the bottom back end of the boat, next to the propellers. The prisoners were divided among ten cells, one of them padded, which opened off an iron gangplank. We managed to scrounge up a .45 pistol for protection. We felt a little more secure having that .45, even though I ended up feeling more sorry for the prisoners than afraid. We split the duties. I was to be on two four-hour shifts—one in the morning and one at night—and we would rotate the shifts. There would be two guards on duty all the time.

If a prisoner had to go to the bathroom, he called out. They could only go one at a time. One of us guards would come down and open the cell door, and the other one would stand at the top of the stairs. We would escort the prisoner to the bathroom. I didn't know where an escaped prisoner could go, but the authorities were afraid that they might get loose and hide on the ship somewhere, then escape once we got to shore.

As we were leaving Liverpool and making our way out through the harbor area, which was not that wide, we saw a huge ship coming in. It was the *Queen Mary,* her decks lined with soldiers. I understand that she carried 8,000 troops. All 300 of us were on one side, and the guys on the *Queen Mary* were waving to us. They were yelling, "How was it? How is it?" And we were yelling back as loudly as we could, "You ain't going to like it! You ain't going to like it!" All those guys were coming over for the invasion. God help them, I wonder what happened to them.

The best thing about that crossing was chow call. Back at the base in England, with all those new crews constantly coming over, getting enough to eat had been a hassle. After we ate, we got back into the chow line because that was the only way we could fill our stomachs. We went into a big cafeteria and ate standing up; then we gave our trays to the garbage detail and went out and got back into line, waiting to eat again.

Not on board this ship. There were so few of us that we all ate in what was normally the officers' dining room. It was a magnificent place. I hung out there whenever I wasn't on guard duty. We had two tables, with tablecloths and napkins and crystal, and a red-headed civilian waiter who worked for the maritime service. He was from New York, a man of about fifty, and he treated us like his own children. The food was amazing: all kinds of meat, chicken, fresh-baked bread and pies. The menu gave us three or four choices, and we could have all four choices if we were so inclined and could manage it. The food seemed incredible to me, a refugee from powdered eggs.

When the boat started rocking, I almost became nauseous and thought I was going to be seasick. But when I saw the food, I put my will to work and said to myself, "You're not going to get seasick!" And I didn't. I never missed a meal.

If it hadn't been for the guard duty, it would have been a less eventful crossing. But the guard duty turned out to be interesting. I got to know some of these bad guys. Kelly, who was only nineteen years old, had stolen an airplane along with another man who could fly. They had flown to Ireland, where he had committed bank robberies and been caught. Now he was headed for a sixty-year sentence in Leavenworth Prison. Another prisoner, an Italian-American, had killed an English girlfriend. Another one had raped somebody. Yet in spite of their serious crimes, they looked like perfectly ordinary guys to me.

They had one duty every evening. We would take six of them down to the galley, and they would haul the garbage cans to the back end of the ship and dump them into the sea through this big open area. We'd walk behind them and see to it that they performed their duties, then come back and lock them up. We'd bring them their meals and escort them to the bathroom, and that was the extent of the duty. We'd go back up to our splendid dining room, have a wonderful meal for ourselves, and then try to catch some sleep or read a little bit.

Guarding these prisoners, some of the gunners—including me—would talk tough to try to impress these guys. We wanted to convince them that we weren't to be fooled with and that they shouldn't try anything. We bragged about our combat experiences we'd been in and the Germans whom we supposedly had killed and how fearless we were, hoping that if these guys had any plans, this would deter them. I don't know whether it helped, but they didn't cause us any problems.

The room I was sharing with about five or six other guys got very stuffy. So I took some blankets and went up on deck by the hatch and for about two or three nights, when the weather wasn't too bad, I slept outside. Then early one morning—it was still dark—I woke up soaked. We were running into heavy seas, and the waves were breaking onto the deck. I went down and dried myself off. For the rest of the voyage I slept in the cabin.

The ship was beautiful. It had all kinds of wonderful warm wood inside. There was a big hallway with a grand staircase up to the next deck. One night we watched an old prewar movie which had a scene with all these people in evening dress boarding a ship and having their going-away parties. The officers were in crisp new uniforms and the women wore lovely gowns. People on the pier were waving to the passengers on board, who were throwing confetti down toward the pier. Suddenly the name of the boat was flashed on the screen. It was the *George Washington,* the same boat we were coming home on. The shots of the boat's interior with all the luxury fittings and furniture and stewards serving drinks was quite a contrast to our present reality. The inside of the ship had been stripped to make room for as many troops as possible.

Every night as it got dark, the Lord's Prayer would be read over the intercom. It was reassuring to hear that. The seas were getting extremely high, and the boat was pitching and tossing. One night all the boat's engines stopped dead, and we were just wallowing in a trough. I was thinking it would be hell to be sunk by a U-boat after surviving twenty-five missions in a B-17.

Talking to the Navy crews who manned the anti-aircraft guns, I found out they'd been on board the *George Washington* for about a year and had made ten crossings. It was good work except for these terrible seas, especially in the dead of winter when the North Atlantic got rough. Then the crews could get cold and wet, and it was not a pleasant duty.

The Cold Blue Sky

At last there came the day we were told we would dock in New York. Until then we hadn't know whether we were going to Boston or New York. We were relieved from guard duty, and the prisoners were locked up to await disembarkation and the M.P.s who were going to meet them. I was glad to be finished with that duty, yet I felt sorry for these guys. We were coming home to freedom, and they were coming home to long stretches in prison.

Finally, there in the distance was the New York skyline. I had never seen New York before. My heart started thumping away. Slowly coming into view was the Statue of Liberty. A ball turret gunner beside me said, "That's Staten Island." He started crying. He could see his house from the boat, and tears were gushing from his eyes. I began to get emotional, too.

Then the tugboats were goosing us onto the pier and there was a military band playing. There were no crowds there to welcome us, only nurses, medical personnel, and a couple of Red Cross workers to take the wounded. But there was a little Army band playing "Roll Out The Barrel." I couldn't believe it. We were back in the United States.

★   ★   ★

After we disembarked, we were put on a ferry and taken over to Fort Hamilton in Brooklyn, where we were going to be processed. Those who wanted could have a pass into New York City that evening. Three other gunners and I decided we would go into town for dinner. We were given instructions on how to get there.

There was a subway station not too far from Fort Hamilton. It was strange walking through a neighborhood that hadn't been bombed. We walked past a group of young guys not in uniform who were our age, or my age anyway. They looked at us belligerently. It was an odd feeling, and my gunner friends felt it too, like being strangers in our own country.

One of the sergeants with me was missing an ear; it had been shot off and his other ear had been frozen. Another had a dangling hand and would probably be discharged. Compared to them and all the other wounded I had seen—not to mention the dead—I felt that I had gotten off very lightly in combat.

We rode the subway, got out at Times Square, and popped up onto the street. I was dazzled. All the lights and neon signs were blazing and blinking. It had been well over a year since I'd seen city lights; wartime London was always dark at night. It seemed as if the war had completely passed New York City by. The streets were choked with cabs, cars, and trucks; wasn't gas rationed? The restaurants were full of food displays. All the vendors had merchandise to sell. I could not believe this was wartime America!

For a while we gawked at the lights like a bunch of hicks. Then we started to look for something to eat. We were all from the Midwest or Texas, and none of us knew anything about New York. We saw a restaurant that looked good. The tables and chairs looked clean, and the waiters were men; in those days, that suggested the restaurant was good. We went in and ordered steaks, which turned out to be both too expensive and so tough and greasy that none of us could eat them. Disgusted, we took the plates up to the counter, left our money with the cashier, walked out onto the street, and went back to Fort Hamilton to get some military chow.

After dinner I went to a phone booth to call my family. They didn't know I was coming home. The phone rang and my dad answered. "Hi, Pop," I said.

"Hello?" he said again, and I repeated, "Hi, Pop."

"Oh my God, it's you," he said and started to cry. Then he said, "Mom went away. She's playing gin with some friends. She'll be sick to hear she missed your call."

I said, "Pop, don't worry, I'll be seeing you. I don't know when, but it won't be too long. I'm in New York, and I'm perfectly safe and sound and well. Give my love to everybody, and I'll be home soon."

The next day we were given our orders. I was going to Fort Sheridan, Illinois, just outside Chicago, for seven days' leave. Then I was to report to Miami Beach for rest, rehabilitation, and reassignment. A new Army program had just been set up to bring all returning soldiers, at this time mostly Air Force combat veterans, to resort environments—Miami Beach in the East or Santa Monica, California in the West—in order to rest up and be thoroughly examined for health and psychological problems by panels of doctors.

The Cold Blue Sky

I took the train to Chicago, went to Fort Sheridan, and was immediately given a pass to visit my family. I rode the elevated train from Fort Sheridan to Chicago and got off at Division Street. It was rush hour, and along came a trolley packed with people coming home from work. I was in uniform, wearing my wings, my sergeant's stripes, my Purple Heart, my Distinguished Flying Cross, and my other ribbons, but nobody gave me a second look. I don't know what I expected. I guess I wanted people to acknowledge me in some way, even to come up and shake my hand and thank me. But they looked right through me. Because of this experience I can relate to the Vietnam veterans who not only weren't recognized, but who also had all kinds of abuse heaped on them. In World War Two most of us returning soldiers weren't greeted with parades, either. Life in America was just going on. No one seemed to give a damn.

I pushed my way onto the streetcar and held on as it lurched forward. Then I heard somebody calling my name. I turned and saw two girls coming towards me. One of them was Naomi. When I was about fifteen or sixteen, we had crushes on each other, but our lives had gone their separate ways. Naomi was still a very pretty girl. She was coming home from work with her girlfriend. She told me that she had read all about my exploits in the newspaper and said she would come over later to talk.

I got off the trolley at Division and Rockwell and looked around. It was still the same old neighborhood; nothing seemed to have changed. The March weather was cold, and I shivered as I walked to the apartment building where we lived. I climbed the stairs to the third floor and knocked on the door of our flat. The door opened, and there were my mom and dad and sister and my little niece Marlene. We all cried. Then I looked around and saw that all my relatives were there: cousins and uncles and aunts and nephews, about twenty of them, all sitting around in our tiny living room, smiling at me and shaking my hand as I made my way around the circle.

I sat down, and everybody looked at me. I guess they were waiting for me to tell them war stories. But I wasn't ready to do that. Besides, I didn't think they would be able to comprehend what I had been through. I tried to answer their questions as best I could, but I felt awkward. Then the doorbell rang, and in walked

Naomi and her friend. They sat down, and we talked about old times and old friends, which was a little easier for me.

Eventually I excused myself, saying I was going to take a walk. What I wanted to do was walk down to Augustus Boulevard where an old girlfriend lived. Just before I volunteered for the Army, I was going with Natalie, a sweet, pretty Polish girl who worked as an elevator operator at the Palmer House Hotel. When I was first in the service, we wrote each other at least once a week. With time we grew apart, but we still wrote letters every month or so. For some reason I wasn't sure about, I wanted to see her, just to say hello and see what she looked like.

Before I left, I told my mother of my feelings about Natalie, who was a Catholic. My mother looked at me and said, "Son, I would rather you marry a Jewish girl, but if you really like her and she likes you and loves you, then it doesn't matter to me as long as you're happy." That was quite a statement from an immigrant Jewish lady, Orthodox in background, who had never known anyone but Jewish people her whole life. My mother was a marvelous woman.

Anyway, I walked over to Natalie's house. I didn't know if she'd be home. She didn't even know I was back in the States. Her mother answered the doorbell, and I saw the same apprehension in her eyes that had been in my mother's. Natalie was home, and we sat and talked, but soon I sensed that we had gone our separate ways. She was glad to see me, but without saying much, both of us knew our relationship was over. Perhaps this was why it was important to see her again. I wanted to be sure our relationship was finished. I couldn't walk away from it without being sure.

My relatives had already left by the time I got back home. The next day, I went out to see some of my friends, like Dave who never went into the service because he had a pierced eardrum. Most of the other guys were in the service. My mother told me about the son of the owner of the little jewelry store on Division Street around the corner from us. The son was a navigator in the Eighth Air Force and had been killed in action about three months earlier. So I went over to the store—his parents knew me, of course—and talked to them about their son and what they'd heard and what mission he'd gone down on and so forth. There was not much I could do except to tell them I was sorry.

The Cold Blue Sky

During the next few days, I walked around the old neighborhood, bought myself a corned beef sandwich, and went to Flukie's and had one of their famous hot dogs. I also saw a couple of my old girlfriends. I guess there was a man shortage, because every gal I met offered me her body, her soul, anything! They just wanted male companionship. There were no young guys around—at least in my neighborhood, there weren't.

Then, before I knew it, it was time to leave for Miami Beach. My parents were worried about me. They didn't believe me when I insisted I was going to stay in America. The D-Day invasion had not yet taken place, there were still lots of air crews dying, and they were terrified that I would be among them.

Chapter Twelve

I caught the train to Miami Beach, where I was assigned to the President Madison, a small six-story hotel right on the beach. I couldn't believe how mellow Miami Beach was, with its sunny weather and fine white beaches.

I bought some bathing trunks. I was no swimmer, but it was delightful to splash around in the surf. After I dried off, I went across the street with one of the returnees I'd met—another gunner—to a little patio where they were selling drinks and snacks. We sat among the coconut palms and drank beer.

Suddenly I saw a tall guy coming down the street with a girl on each arm. "My God!" I exclaimed. "That's my pilot, Tolbert!" I ran across the street. "Captain!" I called. He grinned and said, "How are you, sergeant? It's great to see you." As usual, Tolbert was three sheets to the wind but still under control.

He introduced me to the girls and said, "This is the bravest kid I know. I want to tell you a story about him." He described how as captain of the plane, he had my service records and noticed that I had been disqualified for airsickness. I didn't know that it was still on my record. Tolbert decided he was going to keep an eye on me because if I got sick, I wasn't going to be any good to him or to the crew. The very first time we went up, he watched me throw up into my hat and toss the hat out of the hatch; afterwards, neither of us mentioned it. Tolbert made me feel like a hero for going through with it and trying to hide my illness from him and the crew. I said, "You know, that was the last time I ever threw up."

I never saw James Tolbert again. While I was writing this book, I tried hard to contact him—or anyone in Oklahoma who knows of him—but without success. He was quite a guy and one hell of a pilot.

The Cold Blue Sky

Being in Miami at that time was just wonderful. Coconut palms and warm water! In England the rain was falling as usual, and in Chicago people were still suffering under snow, sleet, and biting winds. I also preferred Florida's summer weather to Chicago's 100-plus temperatures and no breeze. Even in the summertime, when Florida got sticky hot once in a while, delightful breezes still blew off Tampa Bay and the Gulf of Mexico. And it was always cool flying.

We had an interesting group of combat veterans in Miami Beach. There were guys from U.S. Army Air Forces all over the world—from the Fifth and the Seventh in the Pacific, from the Eighth and Ninth in Europe and North Africa, from the Fifteenth which had recently been formed in Italy. There were a couple of survivors of the famous B-24 raid on the oil refineries at Ploesti, Romania.

Every day we reported for medical tests. Most of us had an increased metabolic rate. The medics blamed it on the pure oxygen that we'd been breathing. Maybe that was why we were all so fidgety. After extensive psychiatric and medical evaluations before a board of doctors, I was told that my records were being stamped as qualified for high-altitude aerial gunnery and combat. I looked at them and thought for a moment that I was being given orders for more combat.

In fact I was being reassigned to the Second Air Force, which was headquartered at McDill Field in the Tampa-St. Petersburg area. I was going to be a gunnery instructor. My responsibility would be what they called second- and third-phase training, just before the crews went overseas and were assigned to Eighth Air Force bomb groups as replacements. I don't think they were forming many, if any, new bomb groups at the time. The Eighth was still suffering enough casualties that it needed replacements on a regular basis.

McDill Field had thousands of personnel and trainees and a hundred instructors, but only three combat veterans. I was one and —guess who?—Jimmy Spell was another. He had returned from England and had been assigned to my barracks. The third veteran was a pilot from the 96th Bomb Group whom I had known. As time went on, a few more veterans arrived.

I was actually glad to get on a working air base again. My main concerns were to keep flying, not to get airsick, and to be a valuable member of the team. As an instructor I had a great deal of authority over my gunner-trainees, as well as the prestige of being a decorated combat veteran. They paid attention to my lectures, but they also wanted to know about my personal experiences in combat. And of course they asked what it was like being stationed in England: How were the girls, how was the beer, and what was life like on a combat base?

I went on training flights with the crews in three specially-equipped B-17s. There were cameras mounted on all the .50-caliber machine guns. When you pressed the trigger, the camera would take pictures of fighter planes making passes at us. The film was developed the next day, and we would sit down in the screening room and watch it. I gave critiques of the various gunners' shooting, corrected them, congratulated them, or did whatever it took to improve their accuracy.

I usually flew in the lead plane, standing behind the pilot and co-pilot. I was connected by radio to the other three planes and to the pilots of the fighter planes which simulated attacks on us. The training plane in which I flew most often was the famous *Memphis Belle,* the B-17 whose crew was first to finish a tour of duty overseas. Nearly fifty years later, the *Belle* was the subject of a popular book and movie.

We flew over the Gulf of Mexico and the Florida Keys, the Caribbean, and the Atlantic to solve navigational problems. Or we shot at ground targets on some of the little islands out beyond the Keys. We were on duty for six hours a day, and we flew at all hours of the day and night. One day we would fly from midnight to 0600 hours. The next day we'd fly from 0600 hours to noon. The following day we'd go up from noon to 1800 hours, and the day after that from 1800 hours to midnight. After that four-day cycle, we got three days off.

Another gunner and I managed to get the same three days off on a regular basis. We went to the St. Petersburg beaches, and we both turned brown as berries. He taught me how to play tennis. I enjoyed making friends in Florida because there was no immediate chance of losing them in combat—unlike in England, where I became emotionally numb and stayed to myself.

The Cold Blue Sky

Outside McDill Field, I used to see chain gangs working on the streets. A guard with a shotgun sat in a pickup truck watching shackled convicts repair streets and pound concrete. Such was the life in Florida at that time. As I was finishing this book, I noticed that a couple of Southern states reinstituted chain gangs in 1995.

Then there was life on the base at McDill Field. None of the brass had seen combat—not even the base commander, a two-star general, or the operations officer, a colonel. Our superiors told us veterans in no uncertain terms that we were just to do our jobs and not to flaunt ourselves. I don't know if the other men on the base were jealous, but they didn't like us. The only servicemen we got along with were the crews we trained.

The food was the worst I ever tasted in my life—even worse than on our base in England, and that's saying something. One time I went to the mess hall at 0600 hours after flying since midnight, and I swear the eggs and sausages were shining with a green slime. So I went to the P.X. and had a hamburger and a malt. Sure enough, everyone who ate the mess hall breakfast that day came down with ptomaine poisoning. There was no excuse for serving such horrible food.

The base was poorly run, except for the flight line crews—the mechanics and maintenance personnel who took care of the planes —and our own instruction and training. The lower echelons of the services were just awful. Thank God for the saving graces: the P.X. and the pretty girls who worked there.

I had a wonderful flirtation going with one of these gals. Every time I'd come in, she'd lower her eyes and I'd lower mine. I was still a pretty shy guy. I wasn't one to initiate relationships. The girl usually had to take the first step if she wanted to meet me. And to my surprise, they often did. Girls just seemed to attach themselves to me. There were only a few of us surviving combat veterans, and that seemed to count for a lot. As for me, I had just turned nineteen. I was still lean but no longer just a skinny kid. I weighed about 145 pounds, and I'd grown a little bit taller. I was getting tan. I had a new uniform, including an Eisenhower jacket, and for the first time in my life, I thought I looked pretty good.

I was continually getting phone calls from various girlfriends at the base. I got a gold pen and pencil set from one of them. Another girl followed me back to Chicago and practically moved in with my sister because she thought I had been nice to her. She was obsessed. If I was pleasant to her, she took it almost as a marriage proposal. She had her mother call me on the telephone to ask why we weren't getting married. I couldn't believe these things were happening to me. I found the only way I could get rid of her—and this was alien to my nature—was to be tough, even cruel.

My new assignment was almost like being on vacation—except for flying with these green crews. Some of the pilots had only nine or ten hours of multi-engine time, and some of the co-pilots had never even landed a B-17. Some of the flights with these guys were horrendous, almost as scary as combat.

One day I was in the *Memphis Belle,* which was leading our flight of three B-17s over the Gulf. Our pilot and the pilot of the plane on our right wing were playing games, grinning at each other and trying to touch wingtips. That frightened the hell out of me; I knew what sudden turbulence or a downdraft could do while wings were touching. I ordered my pilot to cease and told him that he was endangering both crews and, more importantly, my own life. The two pilots just grinned and kept on doing it.

We survived, but when I got back to the base I was really steamed. The new assistant operations officer who had just arrived was a major and a combat veteran. I went straight to his office, asked permission to see him, and told him what had happened. He said, "Wait here," and he sent an orderly to get these two pilots. Right in front of my eyes, he read them the riot act and told them that they would be busted to buck privates if he heard of any more shenanigans or if they in any way tried to pull rank on me. He said that while they were flying and I was the instructor, no matter what my rank was, I was to be listened to and to be obeyed. It was one of the most gratifying moments of my life.

We trained these crews, then off they went overseas. I often wondered what happened to them. I'm not making light of what they had to go through, but by late spring 1944 the air war in Europe was going better for our side. The Luftwaffe was being driven from the skies. Our bombers had fighter escorts to and from the targets. We were putting many more planes into the air than a year earlier, and bomber crews had a better survival rate.

Except for the moments of sheer fright with these green crews, my life was pleasant and interesting. I flew around the clock, went to the beach, met nice ladies, played tennis, and read about the war. I should have been content, but somehow I wasn't.

Then one day Jimmy Spell, some of the other combat veterans, and I were summoned to the orderly room and handed new orders. We were granted two weeks' furlough, and then we were to report to McDill for reassignment to a crew headed overseas.

It was funny, but I was almost happy to be going back into combat. Except when I was flying or training, I felt like a misfit. I thought the war and the world were passing me by. Maybe I was forgetting the fear and the danger, but I wasn't alone. Many combat veterans back in the States couldn't wait to get back overseas and often volunteered for second tours of duty. Fighter pilots, bomber pilots, and gunners were going back in droves. I don't know the psychology of why they wanted to go back. I'm sure they didn't want to get killed; they had no death wish. I had no idea why, but I was beginning to feel the same way. I even became a little cavalier with some of my girlfriends because I thought going overseas would give me a margin of safety.

As I prepared to go back home on furlough, I planned not to tell my folks that I was going back into combat. I was just going to tell them that I was being reassigned. When I got back to Chicago, I found that my brother Harry had been able to get leave at the same time. This was the first time we had seen each other in three years. We had a grand time together. He was the only one I told that I was going back overseas. I guess I put an additional burden on him, but I had to tell somebody. I had a good time with my family and friends. Then I caught the train back to Florida.

At McDill Field I awaited my transfer overseas. In the meantime the base got a new commanding officer, a general who had just returned from Italy, where he had been in combat with the Fifteenth Air Force. One of the first things he did was to rescind our transfer, saying there weren't enough highly-trained instructors around, and we weren't to go. Just like that. I was disappointed yet relieved.

We returned to a heavy training schedule. I developed a more relaxed attitude. I recalled that in training, many of us had been as cocky as these new crews. We too had felt immortal and invincible. Now I was looking at these trainees with eyes that had seen a great many things happen. I became more accepting of them and tried to be more tolerant than I was when I first got to McDill.

One of the things I liked was the warm weather allowed us to fly in khakis. At most, I would put on my leather flying jacket. It was a luxury to fly without cold-weather gear and without oxygen. But it bothered me that these new crews were not getting any high-altitude training. They had no experience of the cold at high altitude. They didn't know how to use the oxygen masks and didn't know what it felt like to breathe oxygen for hours at a time. Nobody flew over 10,000 feet. There was no practice in high-altitude formation flying. I thought it was strange. The new crews would have to learn all that when they got overseas, but there wouldn't be much time: They started flying their first combat missions about two weeks after arriving in Europe. I made my concerns known to my superiors, but nothing changed, at least not while I was there.

One morning all the instructors were told to put on their Class A uniforms and their neckties and whatever medals they had. All the crews—I think there were nine crews scheduled for this event—were told to spiff themselves up. We were going to fly to Cuba to help celebrate the birthday of the man then in power, Colonel Fulgencio Batista (Fidel Castro's predecessor).

We landed somewhere near Havana and were taken by bus to a large estate which had been set up like a big carnival with food and drinks. All of a sudden, the great man himself appeared. We stood at attention as this short, heavy-set, swarthy man came down the line to inspect us. Batista looked at us and asked a few questions. He asked the combat vets where we had flown. He said about five words to me, and I saluted him and answered. This famous dictator seemed friendly enough. We stayed there for the day eating and drinking Cuba Libres. Some of the pilots seemed too drunk to fly, but somehow everyone managed to get back to McDill Field and land safely. It was a fun day.

Some pilots just have a crazy streak. One day three planes were taxiing before take-off for an afternoon of gunnery over the Gulf. Our pilot and another were trying to beat each other to the runway. We got there first, and when the other guy had to brake suddenly, up he went on his nose, heavily damaging a three million-dollar B-17. All the props and the nose were completely smashed. The crew was lucky there was no one down in the nose section at the time. I don't know what happened to that pilot's career, but it couldn't have been anything good.

That same day, we had just landed after our flight and were walking across the parking area when three planes came in low. As they turned to land, two of them crashed into each other. They were right overhead, and debris rained down all around us. I almost got hit by one of the wheels. I began to think my job wasn't so safe after all.

I was leading a pretty good life. By now the routine was pretty easy. Every couple of months, I got a furlough for at least a week, and I went back home to Chicago a couple more times. But I wasn't content. I still felt somehow alienated and empty. The news that summer was the D-Day invasion, the infantry and tanks slogging on through Normandy and France, and the Eighth Air Force bombing with full fighter escort all the way. It all left me feeling way, way behind. I wasn't doing the job I was trained for.

I told myself that the Air Force needed instructors with combat experience and that I was imparting valuable knowledge to the crews I was training. I was trying to give them an edge, a better chance of survival when they got overseas. But I missed the intense exhilaration of combat, being shot at, being spared, the high of being alive after a tough mission.

When I went home on furlough and visited my civilian friends, I found we didn't have much to say to each other. One friend had just married a pretty girl, and he was extremely jealous of her. When she gave me a friendly hug and peck—perfectly appropriate for her fiancé's best friend—he got angry and accused me of wanting to steal her. That was the last time I ever saw him. I thought it best to stay away from him. And he had been a loyal friend. What a stupid reason to break up a friendship.

On leave in Chicago, I met a couple of old girlfriends and had brief affairs. I had nothing else to do there but see the family and bask in their love, then come back to Florida to my job. Even with my family, whom I loved deeply, I was just going through the motions. My mother and father never questioned me. All they were concerned about was that the war should end and that I should do something constructive, live a normal, happy life, find somebody, and settle down. As for me, I had no ideas for the future—no thoughts at all. I had no thoughts about what the G.I. Bill of Rights might mean, even though the idea of such a bill was being talked about.

One day I got a call to report to the orderly room. There stood one of the fellows who had come back with me on the *George Washington*. After surviving twenty-five missions on his first combat tour, he had turned around and gone back overseas almost as soon as he got to Florida. He told me he had just finished flying thirty-five missions with the Fifteenth Air Force in Italy. (They got double credit for missions flown across the Alps.) He said that it was a snap, that it was nothing like it was when we were flying in 1943—except, of course, for the guys who were unlucky enough to get shot down or shot up or who had to bail out.

In spite of my acquaintance's optimistic report, the air war in Europe remained pretty hot. The Eighth Air Force was bombing all over Germany, and considerable numbers of B-17s and B-24s were still being shot down—usually by flak. Occasionally German fighters, FWs and ME-109s and a few of the new jets, would sneak through and shoot down some of our bombers. It was still a dangerous business.

I heard that in late June 1944 my old 96th Bomb Group had taken part in a historic shuttle mission, attacking the Ruhland oil fields in eastern Germany and going on to air bases behind Soviet lines. The 96th, along with the rest of the 45th Combat Bombardment Wing's contingent, landed in a place called Poltava in the Ukraine. That night, German bombers attacked and caught all the planes on the ground. The Russian defenses were inadequate, and the Germans took their time, destroying eighty percent of the aircraft that were parked there—including nineteen of the twenty-one B-17s sent by the 96th Bomb Group. I've seen pictures of it. Two Americans and thirty Soviets were killed, and more were wounded. Fifty U.S. bombers were destroyed and twenty-nine were damaged. It must have been horrifying. Still, even though it may sound crazy, to this day I'm sorry I wasn't on that mission.

I started thinking that the war might not last all that long. It was late summer 1944. Paris had been liberated, the Germans were retreating, and it seemed like just a matter of time before Hitler fell. I was thinking of what my next step would be. There was talk about crews being siphoned off from their present assignments to switch to B-29s and take part in the bombing and invasion of Japan. The Twentieth Air Force, which would undertake the bombing, was made up exclusively of B-29s. Curtis LeMay, now a general, had recently taken over as its commander. I wondered about getting into B-29s. I had yet to see one. I understood that they were pressurized and heated and had the latest electronic gunnery equipment.

I wish I could have ended the war with the 96th Bomb Group, especially when they flew the great food drops to the Dutch toward the end of the war. In their advance into Germany, our armies had bypassed most of Holland, which the Germans held tenaciously and which they threatened to flood by opening the sea dikes. During the winter of 1944-45, the Dutch were slowly starving to death. Toward the end of the war the Germans finally gave permission through the Red Cross for Allied aircraft to fly food relief. The 96th and other bomb groups loaded their planes with food and flew at low levels into Holland. The German flak gunners didn't shoot at the bomber crews as they dropped tons of food to the Dutch civilians. I would have loved to have been on that mission, for once dropping food and medicine instead of bombs. That would have been a glorious end to the war for me.

Then it was May 1945, and the war in Europe was coming to a conclusion. All of a sudden it was V-E day. Later, we saw the newsreels of New York, London, and Paris with their cheering crowds, but that day nothing happened on our base. No whistles were blowing; it was a quiet day at McDill Field.

The summer of 1945 passed quickly for me. Almost before I knew it, the war in Japan had ended. Soldiers, sailors, and airmen were being discharged on a point system. As a combat veteran with a couple of awards and a Purple Heart, I was eligible to get out fairly quickly. I was sent to Tinkerfield, Oklahoma for my official discharge from the service. While we were going through the process, I was asked if I wanted to stay in the Army. I said no and, like almost all of us, I went into the Reserves. I was told about my benefits, including medical treatment at Veterans Administration hospitals. I was also given a lapel pin to signify that I was no longer in the service. I was now officially a veteran and a survivor of World War Two. Now I would go on with whatever awaited me for the rest of my life.

Chapter Thirteen

I got on with my life. I met and married my wonderful wife, Daniella, a Polish refugee and artist. We have had a wonderful life together. We have two children, a son, Glen, and a daughter, Jessica, and a successful antique business.

After the war I closed the door on the past. For decades I was occupied with making a living, marriage, fatherhood, and all the other problems and joys of civilian life. I thought little about the war, except for the occasional flashback during a movie or while reading a book. I had almost forgotten about my involvement with the Eighth Air Force and the 96th Bomb Group during World War Two. At times I would talk to my wife about it when we were first married, but that was more than three decades ago. By the early 1980s we hadn't discussed it for many years.

In 1982 my wife and I were on a business trip to New York and decided to go to Washington, D.C. for a couple of days. Neither of us had ever been there. We checked into a hotel and toured the capital's many sights. At the Smithsonian I was stopped short by a tremendous war mural. One part of it showed a flight of B-17s under attack. To my surprise, it brought back a flood of memories.

We had rented a car, and on our drive back to New York to catch our flight home to San Francisco, we passed through southeastern Pennsylvania. I suddenly remembered that the ball turret (belly) gunner on our B-17 crew, Ray "Dutch" Eisenhower, lived in Bethel. We stopped there, and I found his number in a directory, reached his wife on the telephone, and drove to his home.

I hadn't seen or heard from Dutch for over forty years and remembered him as a dark, very nice-looking young man of twenty-four. I myself had been just eighteen. We had been good friends even though we argued a lot. He was very straightforward, neat, and methodical. While I was no slob, let's say I was very non-methodical, and that used to get on his nerves. We'd go on pass together, argue, and end up going our separate ways, yet we remained good friends. The last time I had seen him, we had pulled him out of the ball turret where he had spent almost eight cramped hours at temperatures thirty to sixty degrees below zero. His back, legs, and knees had been frozen.

I pressed the buzzer, the heavy screen door opened, and a bent-over old man appeared. I guess he was almost seventy at the time, and I looked at him and just couldn't get over the shock. He looked at me silently for a long time. Then he seemed to recognize me and said, "Jack, come in." He hugged me and cried. We reminisced. He remembered incidents that I had forgotten. My wife and I stayed with Dutch and his wife for the day, went to dinner, and then proceeded on our way.

Since that time, a great deal of my war experience has flooded back. I have been to Eighth Air Force reunions and have even been back to England, where I was stationed, a few times. I first heard about the Eighth Air Force Society in 1988. The society was having a convention in Cincinnati. On the spur of the moment on a Saturday evening, I decided to attend.

I took a red-eye from San Francisco to Cincinnati, got there about 10:00 p.m., and took a cab to the convention hotel. There I found out that the 96th Bomb Group had a hospitality suite. I went up and saw a couple of dozen men wearing caps and jackets that said 96th Bomb Group. I went over, introduced myself as a veteran of the 96th, and met Bob Owens, who was instrumental in trying to find 96ers and put us in touch with each other.

I asked Bob if he knew of anybody at the convention who had any information about Schroeder's crew. Why I picked the name Schroeder's crew I don't know—maybe because it was the most vivid recollection I had at that time. Just then, somebody went by and said, "What do you want to know about Schroeder's crew?"

"I used to fly with them," I said.

"You did?" he said. "And who are you?"

"My name is Jack Novey," I answered.

"Well, God, Jack," he said, "I'm Tex Shields."

I could have fallen over. Tex Shields and Joe Tonko, another guy on his crew, were—besides me—the only ones from our hut at the convention. Along with the survivors from my crew, they were also the only residents of our hut who came out alive. In a four-month period, of twenty-four men in our hut, twelve were killed, two were wounded, one was a mental case, and seven were taken prisoner, of whom two escaped and came back. The only two to whom nothing happened at all were Jimmy Spell and Dutch Eisenhower.

I was surprised when I thought about it, but the last time I had seen Tex was at briefing, before his plane flew away for what I thought was forever. It went down with smoking engines, and we never heard from the crew. We didn't know they'd been taken prisoner. But Tex survived the war with his crew, including Johnny Euhas, our old crew chief who had insisted on going to gunnery school. Tex made quite a name for himself in the P.O.W. camp, where he organized athletic activities and took good care of sick comrades. Jay Epright survived, too. He was the guy who was always telling me he wouldn't make it.

Tex was lucky twice. If you remember, he was the only survivor of Schroeder's crew, whose plane was shot down on that awful mission to Bremen. Tex missed the mission because he had gone to London to bury his friend Mabry. It was worth my overnight trip from San Francisco to Cincinnati just to see Tex. We remain friends to this day.

$$\star \quad \star \quad \star$$

In May 1991 the 96th Bomb Group held a reunion at our old base, Snetterton Heath. A museum of the 96th was to open there as well. When we arrived in England, we were to meet at an airport hotel in London, then go by charter bus the next morning to Snetterton Heath—about a two-and-a-half-hour trip. Reunion headquarters was the Eccles Hall School, which is housed in a building that was our hospital during the war. The organizers did a great job with the reunion and getting the museum open. They included Sherm Small, who became President of the Eighth Air Force Association; the Eighth Air Force Historical Society; and a number of English volunteers—Geoff Ward, Bert Patrick, and the young people, instructors, and headmaster of Eccles Hall School.

The Cold Blue Sky

I was looking forward to going back. I was particularly excited because my old co-pilot, Norman Macleod, was coming. It had been forty-seven years since I had last seen Macleod. He was the guy whose ears turned red when anything disturbed him. They were my own personal signal: the deeper the hue of red, the more danger we were in. I never told him that until this reunion. It was great to see the others who were there: Tex Shields, Doc Hartman, the old Catholic chaplain of the 96th, and some of the ground crew. I had a wonderful time with my old comrades in arms and their wives and families.

Our reception in Norwich was wonderful. We were welcomed to the Hotel Norwich and installed in our rooms; then we all had lunch in the dining room and went to the bar and drank and talked and told stories. We spent the night there and then drove down to the old base the following day. We had a rollicking bus trip to Snetterton Heath. Our weekend program included a couple of dinners and a lunch with some of our English friends.

The highest-ranking officer attending was Major General Alan A. Rogers, who was on assignment to N.A.T.O. He gave a fine speech. Before taking the N.A.T.O. post, Rogers (then a colonel) had been the commanding officer of the 96th Bomb Group.

The next day there was a moving ceremony at the old Quinham church, right across the road from our base, where Kelley and I, many years earlier, had sought shelter from the rain and had ended up looking at the old tombstones. Lots of local townspeople attended the ceremony. Some were children when we were there. Then we went over to the Eccles Hall School, our old base hospital.

Reporters from the local Norwich paper interviewed and photographed us. At one point I was standing with Doc Hartman, looking at the new museum of the 96th Bomb Group. I pointed at the school said, "Doc? If I'm not wrong, there's the hospital over there to the right."

He said, "That's right."

"Then this building here can only be one building."

Doc asked, "What building is that, Jack?"

I said, "It's the morgue. Our museum is our old morgue." And he agreed. The newspaperman heard me and incorporated my remark into his story.

We went into the museum and looked at the exhibits: old mementos and uniforms and photographs. It was small but quite well done. The next day we went to the Cambridge American Cemetery at Madingley. The cemetery was beautiful: rolling hills, immaculate lawns, beautiful monuments dedicated to the personnel of the U.S. Army Air Forces who died in England, a huge wall with the names of those who were killed or missing in action, and thousands of crosses and Stars of David for those who died and were brought back to England and this, their final resting place. At a dramatic moment, six jets from a nearby American air base roared low over the cemetery, and our hearts went up in the sky with them. It was a fitting salute shared with old wartime friends.

A couple of days earlier in the Norwich Hotel bar, after both of us had had several Scotches, I asked our old chaplain the eternal question, "Why did we make it and the others didn't?"

His answer was short: "How the hell should I know?"

★   ★   ★

In 1994 the veterans of the 96th met at Dyess Air Force Base, where the present-day 96th Bomb Group and 337th Bomb Squadron are stationed. The base is located right outside of Abilene in West Texas. Tex Shields organized this wonderful reunion, and we were shown lots of Texas hospitality.

We visited the base and had a wonderful barbecue at the hangar. It was gratifying to see that they had a B-17 there along with a B-52. Today they're flying B-1 bombers. I met and talked to some of the young pilots and navigators from the 337th and the 96th. We appreciated their interest in us as the original '96ers. It's hard to imagine, but these supersonic B-1s have crews of only four. The planes are controlled by radar and advanced electronics including computers. About all the pilot has to do is to keep his hand on the throttle in case something malfunctions.

★   ★   ★

On Memorial Day 1994 I drove down to a little airfield in Half Moon Bay, about thirty miles south of San Francisco, to see a B-17 and a B-24. One of the veterans' organizations I belong to had informed me that the planes, owned by the Collins Foundation, were going to be there and open to the public for two days. I volunteered to be a sort of a guide and wear part of my uniform. I

175

drove down there and found that the planes were flyable and in good condition, with their guns bristling and a big crowd of people gathered around. A couple of veterans who were already there gave me a badge and told me to help the crowds along and be informative. It was exhilarating, and good for my ego, to have all these people—ranging in age from young kids to fellow World War Two veterans—ask to be shown what I had done and where in the plane I had flown. Many asked me lots of questions about the war. It was a tremendously exciting day for me—so much so that it led directly to my decision to write this memoir.

★   ★   ★

In the process of writing this book, I found out about another old friend: the *Black Hawk*. Our old plane kept on flying for months after I left England. But then it was chosen for an "Aphrodite" mission. Allied intelligence knew about German preparations for rocket attacks on London. French underground forces had informed the Allies that large, elongated concrete bunkers were being constructed near the Channel coast. Our aerial photos also showed the construction of the sites, which we knew were for launching rockets—V-2s at first; perhaps even larger rockets later.

The heavy concrete structures at the launch sites did not seem to be much affected by conventional bombing, and their dense concentrations of anti-aircraft guns were taking a heavy toll of our bombers and crews. So the brass decided that the best way to knock out these launch sites was to strip down older, war-weary B-17s, load them up with 500-pound bombs, napalm, and other explosives, and attack the launch sites with them.

A volunteer pilot and an explosives expert would fly the "drone" plane and bail out before it reached enemy territory. The unmanned drone bomber would then be guided by radio control from a B-17 or B-24 following closely behind. This was extremely dangerous, because the sites were heavily defended. (Among the pilots who lost their lives on these missions was Joseph Kennedy, Jr., the older brother of John F. Kennedy.) The *Black Hawk* was chosen to be one of the drone planes, and it was destroyed on a mission. I don't know whether it hit the target.

★   ★   ★

Looking back, I often wonder just how effective our bombing was and what role we played in bringing the war to an end. We lost an awful lot of good men. I can't help wondering whether our huge loss of life was worth it from a pragmatic standpoint. Did we hasten the end of the war? Would the war have lasted longer had we not flown so many missions with such terrible losses?

Military historians and analysts say we did hasten the end of the war by bombing ball-bearing plants, aircraft factories, and other heavy industry. They also say that the sheer numbers of German aircraft we shot down as they attacked us also helped. They point out that when the Normandy invasion was launched, we had the skies pretty much to ourselves. Many of those ME-109s and JU-88s shot down by our bombers or our fighter escorts would have challenged the Allied invasion on the open beaches, with potentially devastating results.

I am not so sure about the civilian targets we were ordered to bomb. Just as Londoners became even more resolute because of the German bombing, our bombing of German cities may have backfired. But those who made the decision at the time believed that the German civilian population should be given a taste of the horrors of war that their bombers had brought to British, French, Dutch, Belgian, Polish, and Russian civilians.

★   ★   ★

As I think back on the war from the perspective of half a century, my memories unroll like a long film. It's as if I sat through a marathon movie and then walked out of the theater and back onto the bright streets of America. But then I look in my scrapbook, and I see the photos of my buddies and comrades in arms, and I know it all did happen. The photos show boys in uniforms. We were all so young. We were just boys—the boys of *Black Hawk*.

Eighth Air Force Letter to Saint Peter

Let them in, Peter, they are so tired;
Give them the couches where the angels sleep.
Let them wake whole again to find new dawn fired
With sun not war. And may their peace be deep.
Remember where the broken bodies lie . . .
And give them things they like. Let them make noise.
God knows how young they were to have to die!
Give swing bands, not gold harps, to these our boys.
Let them love, Peter — they have had no time —
Girls sweet as meadow wind, with flowering hair
They should have trees and bird song, hills to climb —
The taste of summer in ripened pear
Tell them how they are missed. Say not to fear;
It's going to be all right with us down here.

Index